SECRET SY

of the

Rosicrucians

of the

16th and 17th Centuries

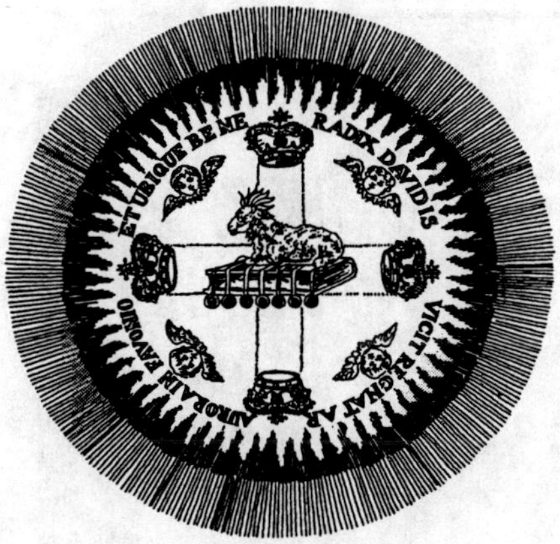

"A Brother of the Fraternity"

ISBN 0-7661-0728-0

The Teachings of the Rosicrucians
of the 16th and 17th Centuries

— OR —

A Simple ABC Booklet

For Young Students

Practising Daily in the School of the Holy Ghost

MADE CLEAR TO THE EYES BY PICTORIAL FIGURES

For the Exercises of the New Year

— *IN THE* —

Natural and Theological Light

by a Brother of the Fraternity { CHRISTI / of the Rosy-Cross } P. F.

FOR THE FIRST TIME MADE PUBLIC

and

WITH SEVERAL FIGURES OF SIMILAR CONTENT ADDED BY P. S.

ALTONA

Printed and Published by Joh. Dav. Ad Eckhardt, Book-Printer to H. M. the King of Denmark

Proverbiorum
27. *v.* 7.

The full soul loatheth an honeycomb; but to the hungry soul every bitter thing is sweet.

ibidem 14. *v.* 6.

A scorner seeketh wisdom and findeth it not; but knowledge is easy unto him that understandeth.

The Almighty, Alone-Wise, and Omniscient GOD and LORD hath given understanding to Man, above all other creatures, so that he may know his works and not leave them unexplored. Now since this Man, whom the All-wise GOD hath inspired thereto, hath this high and profound secret Work and the great secret of the ancient *Water-Stone of the Wise*, he must needs prove himself aright If ever there is a natural thing on earth, it is the Preparation and the *Magysterium* of the Philosopher's Stone, natural and not of man's making, but wholly the work of Nature, for the *Artist* addeth nothing thereto. Nature alone directeth the growing, as doth every tiller of the soil with his fruits and plants; only he must be subtle in mind and have the grace of GOD, so that he may direct the same as the work becomes evident in the boiling and through *successive* time: namely, in the beginning there is the *Subjectum*, which one doth receive from Nature directly into the hand. Therein lieth hidden the Universal Tincture of all metals, animals, and plants It is a rough *Corpus*, having neither the figure nor form of an animal or plant, but is in the beginning a rough, earthy, heavy, viscous, tough and nebulous substance on which Nature hath stopped; but when the enlightened man openeth these matters, investigateth them in *Digestion*, and with its thick foggy shadows with which it is surrounded, he purifieth and permitteth the hidden to emerge, and through further *Sublimation* its innermost soul, which is hidden therein, is also separated from it and brought into a bodily form Then one will find what Nature hath hidden in such a once shapeless substance and what power and *Magnalia* the Supreme Creator hath given to and implanted in this *Creato*. For GOD hath this *Creato* for all other creatures, as in the beginning of creation this power was implanted, and He still giveth it daily, so that it would otherwise not only be impossible for a ma to bring such natural work to the desired end, much less t create herein anything useful. But the good and graciou GOD doth not begrudge man the treasures and goods whicl He hath implanted in Nature, else He would not have grante such things to His creatures; nay, He hath created everythin good for man, and hath made him to be Lord over His cre ation Therefore it is fitting for man to understand and t undertake such a natural philosophical work, for otherwis such a highly-gifted and wonderful creation would have bee in vain, and we would view Nature like the dumb animal which run about, and we would go vainly after God's counse and we would not fit into the ends of Nature *Deus autem e Natura, nihil faciunt frustra* (But God and Nature do noth ing in vain). But GOD Almighty ruleth in all such things He ordereth and provideth that oats and fodder be place before the ass and the horse, but that the rational human bein be served with more costly and more delicious food There fore those who try to investigate and who long for such deeply hidden *Arcanum* and great treasure, in the proper way do not have to depend upon the harvest of the ignorant, wh have no understanding under the Light of our Sun

The *Philosophers* and wise men, as well as *Neoterici* an *Veteres*, have had many disputations about this secret art, an have tried to point out, with many different names, allegories and wondrously strange sophistical words what that *Subjectun* and its *Essentia* are, and what kind of a *Materia*, what kin of a *Corpus*, what kind of a *Subjectum*, and what a wonder ful thing and secret a *Creatura* it is, which hath embodied suc mighty, strange, and heavenly powers, and with which, afte *estion* and purification, one can help human beings, animals, its, and metals, and one can bring their health and perfecup to the highest degree, and one can also do many other vellous things with it Nevertheless all those who were still are true *Philosophi*, have unanimously pointed out single *Scopum* and one only *Materiam*, the *Filii Sapientiat*, ting various and manifold speeches and scripts about it ıcerning the essential thing, however, there is only silence, that silence hath fast-locked their mouths, and placed a d *Sigill* upon them, for if it should become as common knowje as brewing and baking, the world would soon perish

There are many who have searched for that only *Res*, ch *solvit se ipsum, coagulat se ipsum, se ipsum impraegnat, ·tificat et vivicat* (dissolveth itself, coagulateth itself impregeth itself, killeth and bringeth to life again), but most of se searchers, who have lost themselves while searching, ed. Then it is such a thing as is nearest gold; and it is h a thing as the poor as well as the rich can gain, be it atever it may But it threateneth the *Philosophi execrationem inam*, and invoketh the curse of God upon him who with own mouth might *expressly* speak on this *Subjectum*.

When the Philosophers pronounced an *Execration*, nighty God did respect and grant their appeal, and gave o them what He had until then kept in His own hands for eral thousand years Now the aforesaid *Subjectum* is of such nature that it, our *Magnesia*, doth not only contain a small portioned *quantity* of the universal *Spiritus Vitalis* in itself, also hath some of the heavenly power condensed and comssed within it Many who found it were so intoxicated its fumes that they remained in their place and could no ger raise themselves Only a wise man and one who knoweth se things can take a measure of this same fluid and carry nome from whatever place he may have found it, be it from depths of the mountains or any other place where it may met. The poor and the rich are quite free, by the singular d abounding grace of God, to take this, so that he goeth meward with it to his house, and placeth it behind the furce or in any other room where it pleaseth him, and where is convenient for him, and he may begin to work and to periment with it, for he can leave off so quickly that even own servants do not notice it For it doth not go so slowly with this natural work as it doth with the common alchems with their bungling work, with their charcoal-burning, elting and refining, and whatever more they may do But s a work which one can keep in a closed casket in whatever om he wisheth, alone that not even a cat come upon it, and, ould it be necessary, he can well carry on his craft, only ing care that the furnace have a threefold testing, and that keep it at the right heat, and let Nature takes its own course. hen finally the *Solution* is taken out of the *Terrestriaet*, and strengthened by long *Digestion*, it is set free from the *Crudae ateriae*, and is prepared and reborn in the most subtle form. bsequently, of course, this sharp and potent *Spiritus* is at tain times given a well-measured *quantity*, after the fashion drinking and nourishing, *per modum inbibitionis et nutritionis*. d its potency is thus condensed and daily becometh as new pports for its brethren, and active therein Dost thou indeed nk that one canst bring forth such work and such potency unmeasured hidden intensity, a *Spiritus Vitalis?* The *crudae iteriae* or *Subjectum* cometh from the *Astris* and *Constellation* the heavens into its earthly kingdom, from which is then awn the *spiritus universi secretur* of the Philosophers, which the *Mercurius* of the Wise, and it is the beginning, the eans, and the end, in which the *Aurum Physicum* is deterned and hidden, which the common alchemist thinks to exct out of common gold, but in vain. Meanwhile, the *Phisophi* deal much in their writings with *Sol* and *Luna*, which all metals are the most durable in the △. But this is not be understood literally, for their *Sol* and *Luna*, when they brought to their inner *puritaet*, through true, natural, seem- and philosophical *praeparation* may well be compared with celestial bodies, such as the Sun and the Moon, which th their brightness illuminate day and night, the upper and lower *Firmament*. Therefore these two noble metals, like *Sol* and *Luna* of the Philosophers, resemble by nature the man body, and to him who knoweth how to prepare them rightly and use them wisely they give much health, and except and above this nothing else is to be prepared, but the one threefold point of the *Universalis*, for the *Spiritus* to be found in these two said things produceth consistency, strength and virtue, amongst other things

Now the man pardoned by God can prepare and make ready an object or substance of the above mentioned red or white, of *Sol* and *Luna*, which is called the *Lapidem Philosophorum*, or the very ancient *Water-Stone of the Wise*, from the substance in which God placed such potency at the creation or genesis of the world, or the oft-mentioned materials or *Subjectum* which God, out of love and grace, implanted in the highly-endowed divine man But I believe, therefore, that the divine substance which was left to him in the first *Creation* of the world, of the *Spiritu Vitali*, of the *Inspiration*, hath survived in all kinds of creatures. All received the same *Spiritum* in the aforesaid *Massam*, and firmly secluded in the lowest depths of the earth, and it was indicated and left to the Wise Men to disinter it, to extract it, to use it, and to perform the same *Miracula* with it, through the holy wisdom which is still implanted in it and with which it is supplied daily.

Both substances mentioned above as Sun and Moon or red and white, or rather the *Praeparation* ♀ is and *Mercurii*, are the ingredients in the *Composition* of our *Lapidis Philosophorum*. Now then the *Materia* are in the beginning through sufficient and oft-repeated *Sublimentiones* purified and cleansed, and then weighed carefully, and then soon composed; also thou must not be ignorant of what is the potency and occasion of both of the said ingredients, but thou must know how to arrange both *Pondera, secundum proportionem Physicam* (according to the analogy of Physics), for a good portion of the ☿*ii* is encumbered with a small portion of *animae Solis vel Sulphuris*, and then unite both with a delicate hand, so that finally the *Praeparation* and the most difficult work is completed.

But thou wilt have to know that thou must first tinge thy ☿um with the red *Tinctur*, yet it will not become red *in continenti*, but remaineth white, for the *Mercurius* hath the privilege of wanting to be tinged first before all others. The *Philosophi* also tell what to do in addition with the *Anima solis* of this *Tinctur* of the *Mercurii*, and from whence it shall be taken The *Ferment* of gold is gold, just as the *Ferment* of dough is dough. Moreover, it is the *Ferment* of gold out of its own nature, and then its potency is perfect when it is transformed back into earth. And then this is first the beginning of the Philosophers, the right and true *Prima Materia Philosophorum metallorum* (the first *Materia* of the *metals* of the *Philosophers*). From then on the true Masters, experienced in the Art, begin to stimulate their *Ingeniam* and attain to the Great Work. And then the *Artifex* continues further with such work and, through God's blessing, bringeth it to the end, to which it tendeth and where it is embodied by God, namely, to the highly-blessed Philosopher's Stone. So that from nothing else than *per Spiritum universali Secretum* the true *materia prima Philosophorum* is prepared and made ready. Who now understandeth well this *Spiritum Secretum* understandeth also, without doubt, the secrets and wonders of Nature and hath the perception of the light of Nature. For he is *motus harmonicus Sympaticus* and *magneticus*, from which originates the *Harmonia and Concordantia*, the magnetic and sympathetic power or effect of the uppermost and of the lowermost. But note that the natures of both ingredients are unlike each other in the beginning because of their opposed qualities. For one is warm and dry, the other is cold and moist, and they must of course be united. But when this is about to occur, then their opposed qualities must slowly be changed and equalised, so that neither nature through intense fire divest the other of its potency For thou canst never collect them, because both natures must rise simultaneously in the fire's power. Then the *Discrasia* will be taken from the *Corpori*, and an *Aequalitas* and good *Temperatur* is established, which occureth through a moderate and constant boiling.

For when both of the natures *Sulphur* and *Mercurius* are enclosed in a very narrow space and are maintained with moderate heat, they begin to abate from their opposed character and to unite, until finally they have all the qualities. They become one *Conspiration* and rise at the same time, and certainly at the top of the glass standeth *numero* one. They are ready to wed, and then the bridegroom placeth a golden ring on his bride, say the *Philosophi*. And when thus the *Mercurius* with its *Sulphur*, like water and earth with each other, become duly boiled (and the longer the more) they cast away all their superfluities and the pure parts join each other and dispose of their *corlicibi;* otherwise the impure parts prevent unification and the *Ingress*.

For the *Mercurius*, as the first *Corpus*, is entirely crude and can *per anima* be neither mixed nor perpetuated, for neither *Corpus* entereth the other nor will be united with it either *vere* or *in radice*. But should these things be so helped that a true *Tinctur* will be formed, there must be prepared out of this a new spiritual *Corpus* which cometh forth out of both, for after the purification one taketh the virtues of the other, and out of several become one, *numero et virtute* (in number and power). But if the fire should be much too intense and should not be controlled according to the requirements of Nature, these two above-mentioned would be either suffocated or separated If they did not have their right mode of preparation, they would become either nothing or a spoiled work and a *Monstrum* But when one proceedeth prudently and with a duly tempered heat, then both substances will rise in the *Sublimation* uppermost in the glass or cupola Then when thou pluckest these lovely flowers, thou canst enjoy them already *particularia*

But thou canst observe the *motum occultum naturae* as little as thou canst either hear or see the grass growing, for one can neither observe nor notice the increase and development of these two ingredients, *Mercurii* and *Sulphuris*, because of their subtle, hidden, and slow *Progressus* from hour to hour. Only by marks set from week to week can it be observed and a conclusion drawn, for the inner fire is very delicate and subtle But however slow it may be, it doth not stand still until it cometh to the end where its *intent* is to be seen, as in all plants, unless it then be that such subtle and expert boiling is hindered through the all too-strong heat of the sun and is burnt out, or is hindered through suddenly appearing cold: *ergo qui scit occultum motum naturae, scit perfectum decoctionem* (therefore he who knoweth the hidden movement of Nature, knoweth also the perfect boiling or preparation) This *motum* should now take its natural and self-determined course, although one can neither hear nor see it, as also one cannot comprehend the *Centra et ignem invisibilem seminum invisibilium* (the Centre and invisible fire of the invisible seed) Therefore thou must commit such a matter to Nature alone, and observe it and not once try to oppose Nature, but have all confidence in it until it bringeth forth its fruit

When one treateth Nature with a gentle and agreeable heat, it doeth and effecteth everything out of itself, which for the furnishing of a *Creati* or the introduction of a new form is a matter of necessity: for the Divine Word *Fiat* still abideth in all creatures and in all plants, and hath its mighty power in these times as well is in the beginning

There are, however, four chief *Virtutes* and *potentias* of which noble Nature maketh use in every boiling; thereby it doth complete its work and bringeth it to an end.

The First Virtus

Is and is called *appellativa et attractiva*, for it is possible for it to attract to itself from far or near, food of which it is desirous out of results and places agreeable to its nature, and it can grow and increase. And here it hath a magnetic power, like that of a man for a woman, the *Mercurius* for the *Sulphur*, the dry for the moist, the *Materia* for the form Therefore the axiom of the Philosophers is: *natura naturam amat, amplectitur prosequitur. Omnia namquam crescentia, dum radices agunt et vivant, succum ex Terra attrahunt, atque avide arripiunt illud, quo vivere et augmentari sentiunt* — *i e.*, Nature loveth nature, surroundeth it, and followeth it. For all plants, when they strike root and begin to live, suck sap out of the earth, and draw to themselves avidly that whereby they sense they can live and multiply themselves. For where there is hunger and thirst, food and drink will be received with avidity and this *Virtus* and *potentia* will be aroused, and it cometh from the heat and average dryness.

The Second Virtus and Potentia

Is and is called *natura retentiva et coagulativa*. For Nature not only alone is useful to it and serveth it for its continuation and is advantageous when it lacketh that which it eagerly produceth from itself, but hath also with it the bond with which it draweth and bringeth and holdeth it to itself. Yea, Nature even changeth it into itself, for as it hath chosen of these two the purest parts, it separateth the rest and bringeth to the mouth and maketh it grow, and is in no need of any other *calcination* or *fixation: natura naturam continet* (Nature retaineth nature), and such skill cometh from its dryness, for the cold constricteth the gained and evenly-formed parts and drieth them in the *Terrae*.

The Third Virtus and Potentia

naturae in rebus generandis et augmentandis.

Est Virtus digestiva, quae fit per putrefactionem seu in putrefactione (is the digestive power, which occurs through the putrefaction or in the putrefaction), in moderate and temperate heat and moisture. For Nature directeth, changeth, and introduceth one kind and quality, the crudeness is done away with, the bitter is made sweet, the harsh is made mild, the rough is made smooth, the immature and wild is made tame, that which was formerly incapable is now made skillful and efficient, and leadeth to the final intended execution and perfection of the Work, and representeth the *Ingredientia* to the *Composition*

The Fourth Potentia naturae

Est virtus expulsiva mundificativa, segregativa (the expelling, purifiying, separating power) which separateth and divideth, which purifieth and cleanseth, which washeth during the *Sublimation* or *Decoction* It setteth from *Sordibus* and darkness and bringeth forth a pure, transparent, powerful or illuminated *Corpus* or substance; it collecteth the *Partes homogeneis*, and is gradually set free from the *heterogeneis*, repulseth the *Vitia* and everything alien, inspecteth the crude, and giveth every part a special place This is caused by and cometh from the agreeable constant heat in appropriate moisture, and that is the *Sublimation* and mature fruit, which will now fall out of the husk Therefore it is in the beginning designed by Nature and artisans, namely the *Patiens* is set free from the *Agente*, and will be perfected *Nam liberatio illa a partibus heterogeneis est vita et perfectio omnis Rei,* — *i e*, for the liberation of these unequal and opposed parts is the life and perfection of all things For the *Agens* and *Patiens* which until now have been contending with each other, so that each affecteth and rendereth resistance according to its opponent's resistance — *i e*, as much as possible it would like to break its opponent's resistance and they must not unite during the time of their *Decoction*, but the best part must gain the victory and expell the impure, and subjugate it.

Now when all *Naturalis potentia* have done their *officium*, then cometh forth the new birth and as the mature fruit presenteth itself in all other plants, so also now in our *Subjecto* and natural work which, when perfected, quite surprisingly doth not at all resemble any more its first beginning and hath no more quality, and is neither cold nor dry, neither moist nor warm, and is neither *masculus* nor *foemina* For cold is there itself turned into heat, and the dry into the moist, the heavy into the light, for it is a new *Quinta Essentia*, a *Corpus Spirituale*, and hath become a *Spiritus corporalis*, such a *Corpus* as is clear and pure, transparent and crystallike; one which Nature itself, could never have produced as long as the world hath stood. The *Artifex* and the enlightened man, however, *auxiliante Deo et natura* (by the aid of God and Nature), produceth through his intellect and art, and he placeth it there by itself So that subsequently he encountereth a *Miracula* and that is called: *Unguentum anima, aurum Philosophorum, flos auri* (the unguent, the soul, the philosophers' gold, the flower of gold). *Theophrastus* and others call it *Gluten aquilae*.

Now what is shown about the four *potentiis naturae*.

the same had been effected by means of the fire, which must be incombustible, pleasing to Nature, and according to Nature it must continue steadily and must also be advantageous to the Work: but in this Work two kinds of fires are to be particularly well attended to, namely: the outer elementary fire which the *Artifex* constructeth and which he applieth to the Work, and after that the inner, innate, and natural fire of the substances. Though in all three primary things or genera there is to be found a natural fire as in the *Animalibus, Vegetabilibus*, and *Mineralibus*, through which it started and moved, maintained life, was strengthened and increased; and can continue its innate power of bringing forth and of implanted virtue according to the character of each.

But the fire which is in our *Subjecto* is in itself not least amongst creatures and minerals. It hath hidden within itself the most wonderful, the most potent fire against which the outer fire seemeth like water, for no common elementary fire can consume and destroy the pure gold which is the most durable substance amongst all metals, however intense the fire may be, but the essential △ and ▽ of the Philosophers alone doeth it.

If we had to-day that fire with which Moses burned the golden calf and ground it to powder and strewed it upon the water and which he gave to and made the Children of Israel drink of it (*Exodus*, ch. 32) — let such be a piece of alchemical work of Moses, the man of God! For he was instructed in the Egyptian art and skilled therein. Or the fire which the prophet *Jeremias* hid beneath the foot of the mountain, from which Moses saw the Promised Land and whereon he died, the fire which was recovered seventy years later by the Wise Men, the descendants of the old priests after the return from the Babylonian Captivity But in the meantime the fire was changed in the mountain and became dense water (II *Maccab*, ch. 1 and 2). What thinkest thou? should we not warm ourselves at it and keep from us the frost in winter?

Such fire slumbereth in our *Subjecto* quietly and peacefully and hath no movement of itself Should now this secret and hidden fire help its own *Corpori*, so that is may rise and have its effect, and manifest its might and power, so that the Artist may reach the desired and predestined end, it must be aroused through the outer elementary fire, be kindled and be brought into its course This fire may be in lamps, or of whatever kind thou dost like, or contrive, for it alone is sufficiently capable of executing the activity with ease, and such fire and outer heat must be tended and maintained all the time until the end of the *Sublimation*, so that the inner and essential fire be kept alive, in order that the two indicated fires may help each other and the outer fire let the inner fire be worthy, until in its appointed time it becometh so strong and intense a fire that it will soon burn to ashes, pulverise, turn into itself, and make equal to itself all that is put into it but which is nevertheless of its own kind and nature.

Nevertheless it is necessary for every *Artifex*, at the cost of his desired end, to know that between these two abovementioned fires, he maintaineth certain proportions between the outermost and the innermost, and that he kindle his fire rightly, for if he maketh it too weak, then the Work cometh to a standstill, and the outermost fire is not able to raise the inner one, and in so far as he stirreth it up moderately several times, it yieldeth a slow effect and a very long process, and when he hath waited with such patience and hath his data, he then finally reacheth his intended goal. But if one maketh a stronger fire than befitteth this process, and it be speeded up, then the inner fire suffereth, it is entirely incapable, the Work will surely be destroyed, and the hasty one will never attain his end.

If after lasting *Decoction* and *Sublimation* the noble and pure parts of the *Subjecti* are gradually, with the advantage of a calculated time, separated and set free from the crude earthly and useless substance, the impulse in such activity must be according to Nature and must be adjusted with such moderation that it will be agreeable, pleasing, and advantageous to the inner fire, in order that the inner essential fire be not destroyed through all too-intense heat, or even extinguished and made useless. Nay, rather it will be maintained in its natural degree, be strengthened, whilst the pure and subtle parts come together and convene, the crude being separated, so that they combine and the best will achieve the aforesaid end in view. Therefore thou must learn from Nature that degree of fire which Nature useth in its operations until it bringeth its fruit to maturity, and from this learn *Reason* and make calculation. For the inner essential fire is really that which bringeth the *Mercurium Philosophorum* to *aequalitaet;* but the outer fire stretcheth forth to it a hand so that the inner fire will not be hindered in its operation, therefore the outer must have concordance with the inner and must adjust itself according to the same, *vice versa*. Then in such use of the universal elementary fire it must be led toward the inner natural heat, and the outer heat hath to be adjusted to it, so that such doth not surpass in the *Creato* the power of the moist and warm *Spiritus*, which is wholly *subtil;* if otherwise, the warm nature of the said *Spiritus* would soon be dissolved, and it could not hold itself together any more, and would have no potency; it followeth therefrom that a fire more intense than is necessary for reviving and maintaining the inner natural fire implanted in our *Materiae* can only be for hindrance and deterioration. *In natura et illius Creatis et generationibus sit tua Imaginatio*, — *i.e.*, upon Nature and what hath been created or brought forth by her, mediate thou. Therefore bring the moist *Spiritum* into the earth, make it dry, *agglutinirs* and *figurs*, with an agreeable fire. Thus shalt thou also bring the *Animam* into the dead *Corpus* and restore what thou hast taken away, and thou restorest the soulless and dead to life and to rise again and be equipped, but whatever hath driven it will not stand the heat, for it will not become constant as if it were to be received spontaneously from itself with good will, with joy and with desire, and be deeply impressed.

And that is *sicci cum humido naturalis unio et ligamentum optimum* (the natural unification of the dry with the moist and also the best tie). Yea, if one really desireth to discuss this matter: the Wise Men mention three kinds of fire, each of which taketh charge of the *operis magni*, so that each best form in particular must in wisdom and good readiness have governed this also. And so he will not work as one blind, but in an understanding and prudent manner, as befitteth an intelligent *Philosophus*.

The first is the outer fire, which the *Artist* or watchman maketh, which the Wise Men call *ignem frontem*, upon which *Regimen* dependeth the safety or the ruin of the entire Work, and this in two ways: *nemium sumiget cave* (take heed that it doth not smoke too much), but it is also said: *combure igne fortissimo* (burn it with the strongest fire).

The second fire is the nest wherein the *Phoenix* of the Philosophers hath its abode, and hatcheth itself therein *ad regenerationem*. This is nothing else than the *Vas Philosophorum*. The Wise Men call it *ignem corticum*, for it is written that the *Phoenix* bird collected all fragrant wood whereon it cremateth itself. If this were not so, the *Phoenix* would freeze to death and it could not attain to its *Perfection*. *Sulphura Sulphuribus continentur* (Sulphurs are maintained by sulphurs). For the nest should protect, assist, cherish and keep the brood of the bird unto the final end.

The third however is the true innate fire of the noble *Sulphuris*, itself to be found *in radice subjecti*, and is an *Ingredient*, and it *quieteth* the *Mercurium* and fashioneth it: that is the real Master, yea, the true *Sigillum Hermetis*. Concerning this fire *Crebrerus* writeth: *In profundo mercurii est Sulphur, quod tandem vincit frigiditatem et humiditatem in Mercurio. Hoc nihil aliud est, quam parvus ignis occultus in mercurio, quod in mineris nostris exitatur et longo temporis successe digerit frigiditatem et humiditatem in mercurio*, — *i.e.*, In the essence of the *Mercurii* is a sulphur which finally conquereth the coldness and the moisture in the *Mercurio*. This is nothing else than a small fire hidden in the *Mercurio*, which is aroused in our *Mineris*, and in the fulness of time it absorbeth the coldness and moisture in the *Mercurio* or removeth them, and that is also said about the fire.

FINIS

IF A PHILOSOPHER YOU WISH TO BE,
Where on this globe lives a man so wise,
Who'll ever learn what four ones do comprise,
And even if he'd know all this,
He'd still always be an apprentice.
Therefore, O human, with all thy might,
Recognise God and thyself in God's and nature's light,
Both these lights God pours into thee,
That a likeness of him thou mayest be,
He is one fourfold God, let thou be told,
As thou art a piece of clay fourfold.
This maketh nature to thee well known,
With wisdom, light and understanding to thee is it shown.

LET ONLY PATIENCE DWELL IN THEE.
To nothing can thine eye be blind,
Be it of body or of mind.
Therefore be thankful to thy God,
Who in time this before thee hast brought.
Be thou not jealous of the scoffer's fame,
Do not begrudge every mocker's great name.
With sophisticated vanity they strut,
Unbeknownst to them is what thou'st got.
Be happy with what God to thee gave,
Defy, that four in one they have.
Fiat and Amen, be my treasure,
A fourfold sphere always together.

O DOMINE QUAM MIRABILIA SUNT OPERA TUA.

Lord, thine eternal Spirit is in all Things.

Salvator ☿ Mundi

Four fires are floating in this world,
Wherein God holdeth a Center,
That is locked up in four,
Out of which Heaven and Earth were poured.

SPECULUM DIVINUM OCCULTUM ATOUE

Friend, thoughtfully look at this mirror,
See how nature is revealed,
Always watch the inner center,
Turn the outer spheres around it,
LABORATORIUM PERPETUUM.

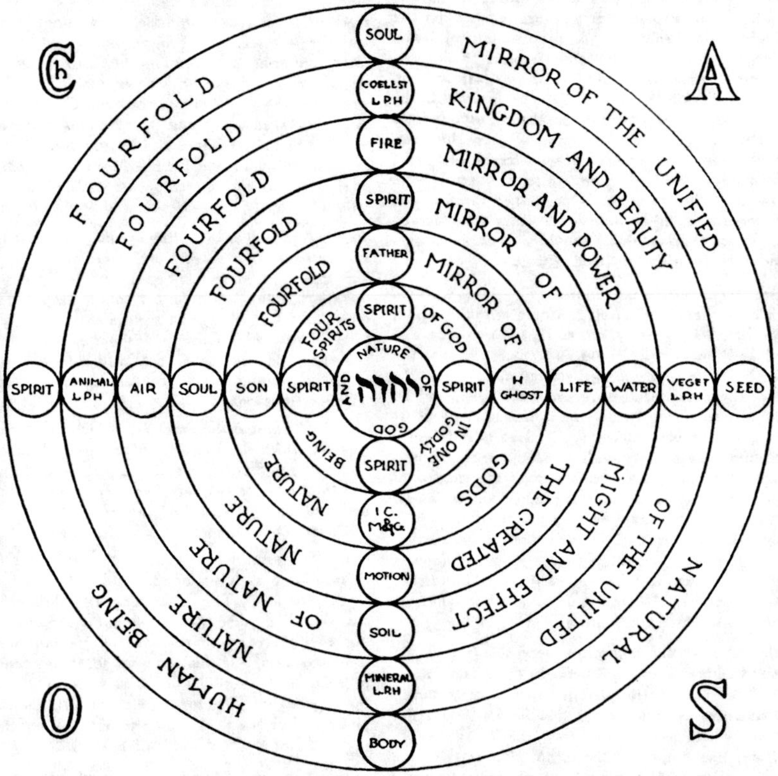

So thou hast all in all,
Earth and Heavens in one together,
Look well at it, it is to thy good,
And pondering over, thou wilt not rue it.
NATURA RERUM SEU INSTRUMENTARUM.

IGNEUM PHILOSOPHORUM ET

Notice Nature in its strength,
Look at its great life-power.
From God it, and all things spring,
And return to their centers again.

Coel. & ☿ Terra.

There is never a Philosopher who Nature's ultimate Principle doth not know.

Look well for the golden Magnet. If thou findest it thou wouldest get rid of thy sorrows.
Study well the law KNOW THYSELF, that thou may not be deceived any more.
Unum sunt omnia, per quod omnia.
Make known to thee the Terra Sancta, so that thou mayest not go astray.

Figurative Image of how within this World three Worlds in each other,

namely this earthly Sun-World, and also the heavenly and

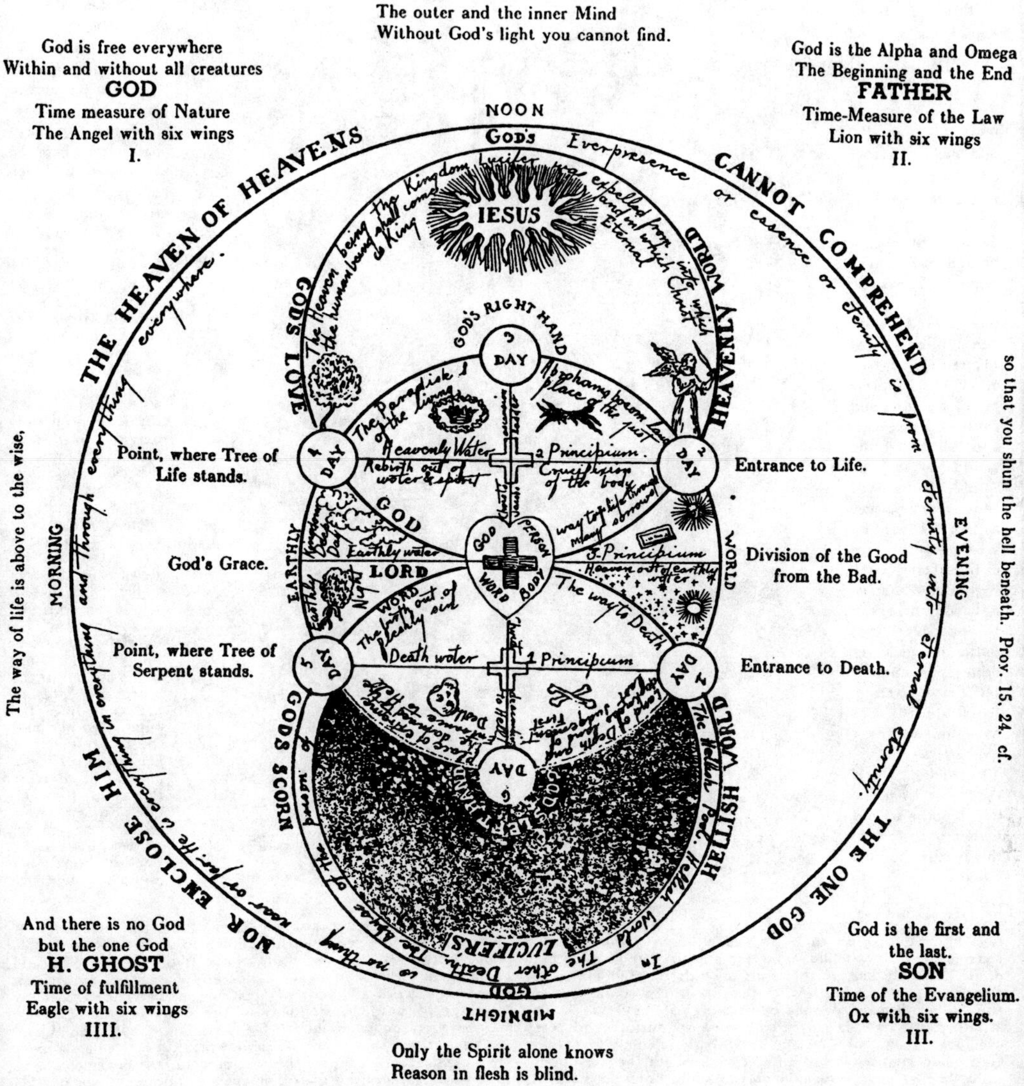

the hellish world have their effects. And the darkness cannot conquer the light. It also shows that the land of the dead, the entrance to hell or superficial darkness, where there is wailing and gnashing of teeth, as well as the land of the living, the heavenly paradise or third heaven are from this world. And that the human being has all these things in his heart; heaven and hell, light and darkness, life and death.

The Tree of Good and Evil Knowledge

THERE IS ONE TREE bearing two kinds of fruits Its name is the tree of ,the knowledge of good and evil Like its name. are its fruits: namely. good and bad fruits of life and death. of love and hate. of light and darkness. This tree was put before Adam. and even if he had in his innocence the liberty to look upon it as a tree of God's wonders God's prohibition did not allow him to place his desire in it and eat of it. but threatened that (if he would do so) he would die from its fruit For this was a tree of division where good and evil battled with each other: but in a battle there can be no life: For battle brings forth destruction, and destruction brings forth death. life lives in the sweet unity of love Therefore. when Adam ate from this tree. a battle started within him. and in this battle he lost his life

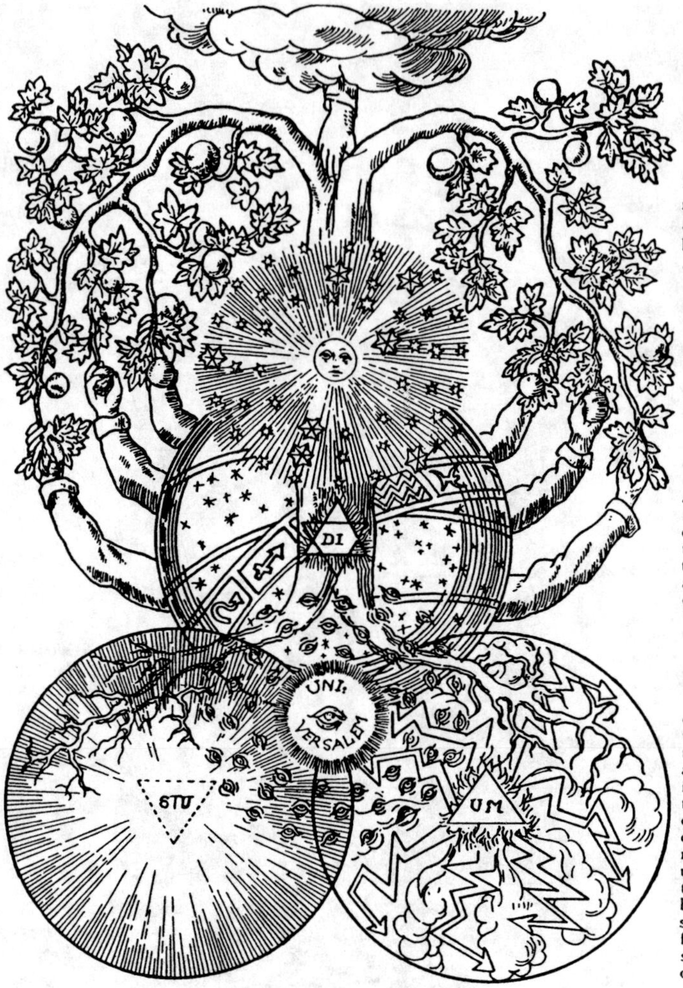

Neverthe-less wretched men will not learn through such fall and damage. His desire is still for that tree and its fruits Man is always desirous to have the division of manifold things. and man is always battling. when he could return to the unity of simplicity. if he only would come in peace Life's light stands in the middle to point out to men the way to this first rest. and the Father in the heaven lets his Sun rise over good and evil: But everything grows after its own fashion. and man is only too apt to look upon the stars of the many-foldness. and in his own discretion. to choose them for his ladders. though they make him stray many times from the true light. and detain him in the whirlpool of uncertainty This whirlpool of uncertainty leads more and more out of the innermost face of the Sun into the outer (world) and can find neither end nor place of rest. unless it leads from the outer (world) back again and seeks the beginning. from which all the smaller star-lights originated

There is also among 7 stars. hardly one turning its rays inward to direct the searching mind to Bethlehem. and amongst 7 eyes winding around the whirlpool of searching desire is hardly one which stands towards the Sabbath in the innermost: but the restless movement of the working days move them through all spheres. and even if they take a look at God s wonders. they only look upon the surface and every eye looks upon that which is shown through its own desire. God made man to live in an eternal Sabbath. he should not work. but let God work in him. he should not take with his own hands. but only receive what God bestowed plentifully upon His mercy But man left the Sabbath. and wanted to work himself. raised his hand against the law to take in his own desire what he should not have taken Therefore. God let him fall. and since he had despised the quiet. he had to feel painfully the restlessness In such restlessness of life all children of man still extend their hands. trying to grasp their pleasures And as is their understanding and will. so is their grasping Some grasp for the good. some grasp for the evil Some grasp for the fruit. some only for the leaves. some for a branch with fruits and leaves on it. And they derive pleasure from the things they have grasped. these poor fools do not know that all their pain and labor had only been a *Studium particulare* They grasp for pieces. where they could obtain the whole They seek for quiet and cannot find it: for they look from the outside into the restlessness of movement. which dwells in the inner solitude of the inner *Centri* and though one may grasp more than the other. it is still piece-work At times there may be one amongst 7 hands coming near the secret and it grasps the whole stem of the tree at that point where all the divided branches return to unity. But even this hand is still far from the roots of the tree. only grasping and holding the secret from the outside and cannot yet see it from the inside For the root of this tree is understood only by the eye of wisdom. standing in the *Centro* of all spheres. These roots go from the visible world of mingled good and evil. into the sphere of the invisible world This eye looks with the greatest peace upon the wonders of all movements and also looks through all the other eyes. wandering about outside of the rest in the unrest. all those eyes which want to see for themselves without the right eye of wisdom. from which they have received all their seeing-power This eye can prove all spirits. how intelligent. pure and acute they be It understands the sources of good and evil Plain before it is light and darkness It understands time and eternity. visible and invisible. present and future things. earthly and heavenly things. things of the body and things of the spirit. high and deep. outwardliness and inwardliness. And nevertheless. none of these things are disturbed by it. for the eye lives in the *Centro* of peace. where everything stands in equality outside of any strife. and whatever it sees it possesses. For in the *Centro* of its peace is its kingly throne. everything being subject to it Therefore. dear man! If thou wouldst return to right understanding and right peace. cease from thy works and let God alone work in thee. so that the eye of wisdom will open in thine own self and thou wilt attain a *studio particulari ad universale* and One find All

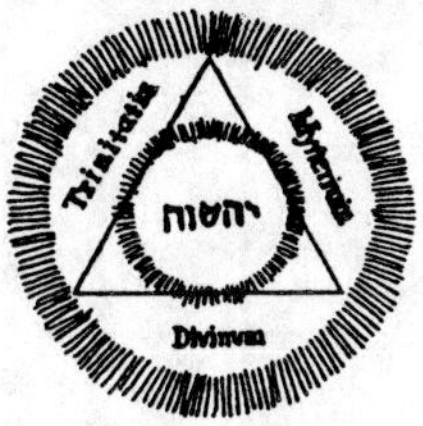

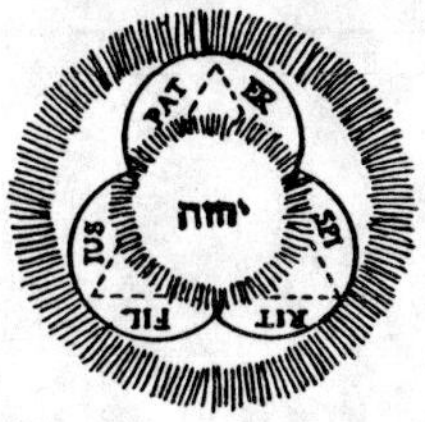

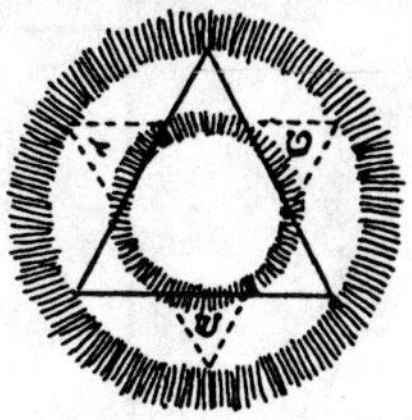

I am the Alpha and the Omega, the beginning and the end, saith the Lord, God liveth in a Light, since no one can come to Him, or near Him.

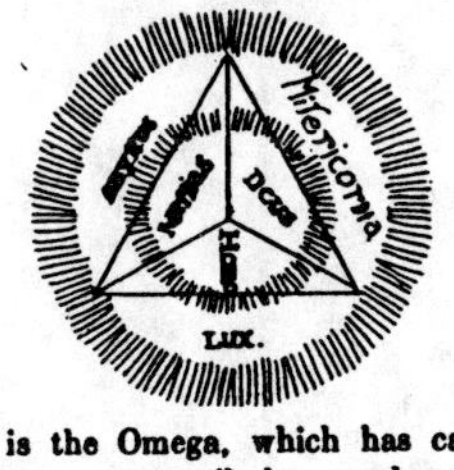

This is the Omega, which has caused so many many evil days and restless nights.

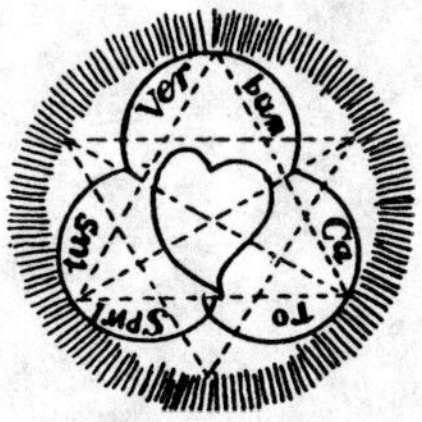

This is the trifling matter over which so many hundreds of people moaned in vain.

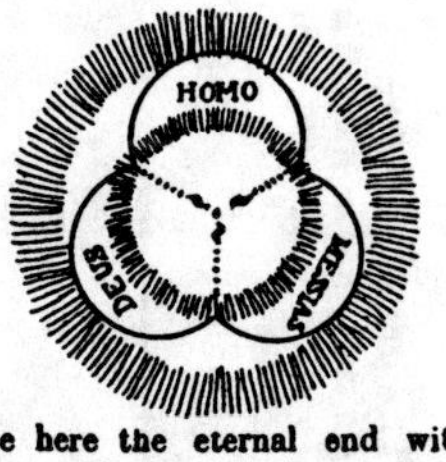

Notice here the eternal end without beginning, the eternal revelation and circle, in eternal love, willpower and centro ⊙ whose principle reveals itself since eternity began.

You will see in this the eternal nature in its seven apparitions, revealing itself in the centro ○ of the eternal bottomless depth since eternity began.

The Centrum of the eternal bottomless depth of light and darkness is in the infinite inexpressable width and depth everywhere. Therefore is said: The light inhabits the darkness and the darkness cannot grasp it.

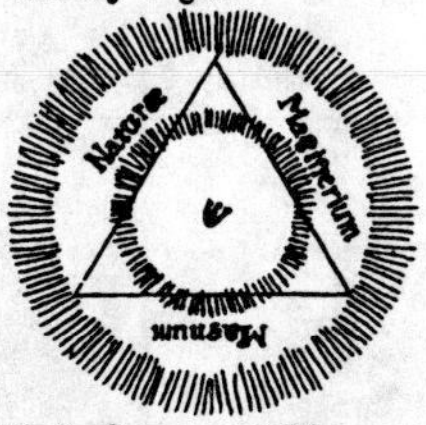

An eternal holy fire
An infinite God sent flame
A heavenly secret

} The great indescribable spirit of fire, inexplorable in eternity.

Harmonious Conception of the Light of Nature.

FROM WHICH YOU CAN DEDUCE THE RESTORATION & RENOVATION OF ALL THINGS EMBLEMATIC.

The art is just, true and certain to the
Man who fears God and is assiduous,
And behaves rightly towards all natures.

The art makes him a lord, not a servant.
Do not make haste, stay on the right track,
So thou wilt have much profit and much joy.

If God grants many things in thy life,
Give plentifully to the poor,
Be faithful and silent about the art,

For this surely is God's will,
Keep truth and faith, think of me,
So thou wilt be free from all evil.

MONS PHILOSOPHORUM.

The soul of men everywhere was lost through a fall, and the health of the body suffered through a fall, Salvation came to the human soul through IEHOVA, Jesus Christ. The bodily health is brought back through a thing not good to look at It is hidden in this painting, the highest treasure in this world, in which is the highest medicine and the greatest parts of the riches of nature, given to us by the Lord IEHOVA It is called *Pator Metallorum*, well known to the philosopher sitting in front of the mountain-cave, easy to obtain for anybody. But the sophists in their sophistic garb, tapping on the walls, recognise him not. At the right is to be seen *Lepus*, representing the art of chemistry, marvellously white, the secrets of which with fire's heat are being explored To the left one can see freely what the right *Clavis artis* is; one cannot be too subtle with it, like a hen hatching a chicken In the midst of the mountain, before the door stands a courageous Lion in all its pride, whose noble blood the monster-dragon is going to shed; throwing him into a deep grave, out of it comes forth a black raven, then called *Ianua artis*, out of that comes *Aquila alba*. Even the crystal refined in the furnace will quickly show you on inspection *Serrum fugitirum*, a wonder-child to many artists The one effecting this all is *Principium laboris*. On the right hand in the barrel are *Sol* and *Luna*, the intelligence of the firmament. The Senior plants in it *Rad Rubeam and albam* Now you proceed with constancy and *Arbor artis* appears to you, with its blossoms it announces now *Lapidem Philosophorum* Over all, the crown of the glory, ruling over all treasures

Be diligent, peaceful, constant and pious, pray that God may help thee And if thou attain, never forget the poor Then thou wilt praise God with the legion of the angels, now and forever

Mercy - Choice.

Light, strength, joy in the recognition of God's virtue and hymn of praise.

Darkness, evil-doing, fear in Godlessness, sin and vice.

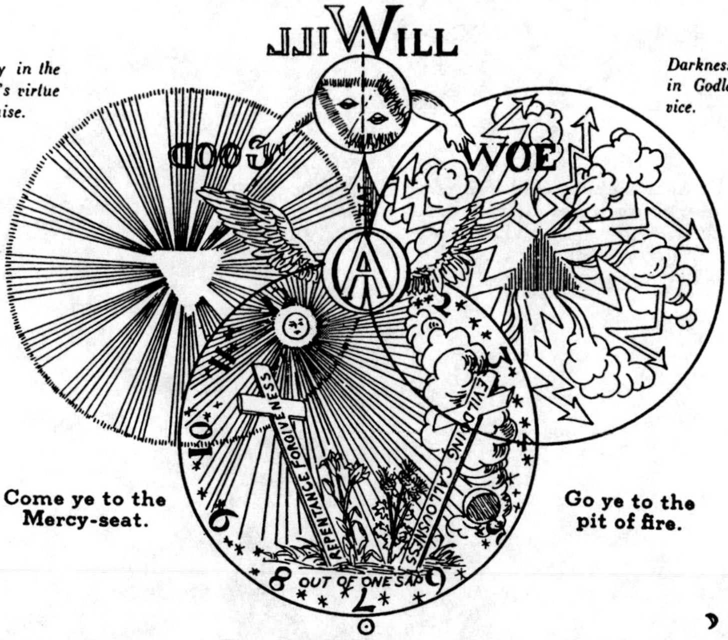

Come ye to the Mercy-seat.

Go ye to the pit of fire.

♄

Harsh, hard, cold, severe, sharp, sour, inclined to rudeness and earthliness, its desire consists out of these qualities.

Fire or life, half in darkness, half in light, is the setting alight and the goal of separation.

☽

The being, made out of the forenamed six spiritual qualities, in which they lie bodily and in readiness, as in their coffer.

♂ Fear, heat, therein consist the sensibilities.

☿ Bitter, drawing and moving out of the harsh quality, which causes a sting within, and remains in that spirit, the existence of mobility.

The first and dark Principium. God the Father, being called a consuming fire.

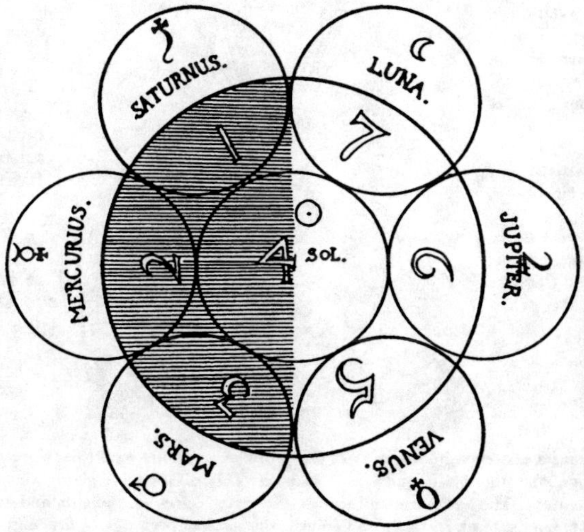

The other Principium of light, being God's Son, is one with the eternal world of light.

♃ Is the power from the life of light, in it is fulfilled God's word of the cognition, sound, call and tone.

♀ Light, love, fire, which burns in the oil of Mercy, in which consists the heavenly life.

The Principium of the fire belongs to the world of the four elements, being an offspring of the first two, and is the third principle.

Whenever the first three qualities of the first dark Principii gain the upper hand, then the others are tied up around their Centro and all seven are evil. Then Saturnus stands for avarice, Mercurius for envy, Mars for wrath, Sol for vanity, Venus for lewdness, Jupiter for cunning and Luna for bodily desire, which are the seven evil spirits ruling within the old human being.

But when the three in the Principio of light have the upperhand and are born out of the dark Centro, so that they are in accordance with their innermost depths of light, which is the new birth in man, all seven are good, and then Saturnus stands for compassion, Mercurius for doing good, Mars for gentleness, Sol for humility, Venus for chastity, Jupiter for wisdom, and Luna for Christ's flesh or body.

The Hermetic Philosophy.

I attract all those seeking God and the truth; those alone will find the art. I am the Magnet-Stone of divine love; attracting the iron-hard men on the road to the truth.

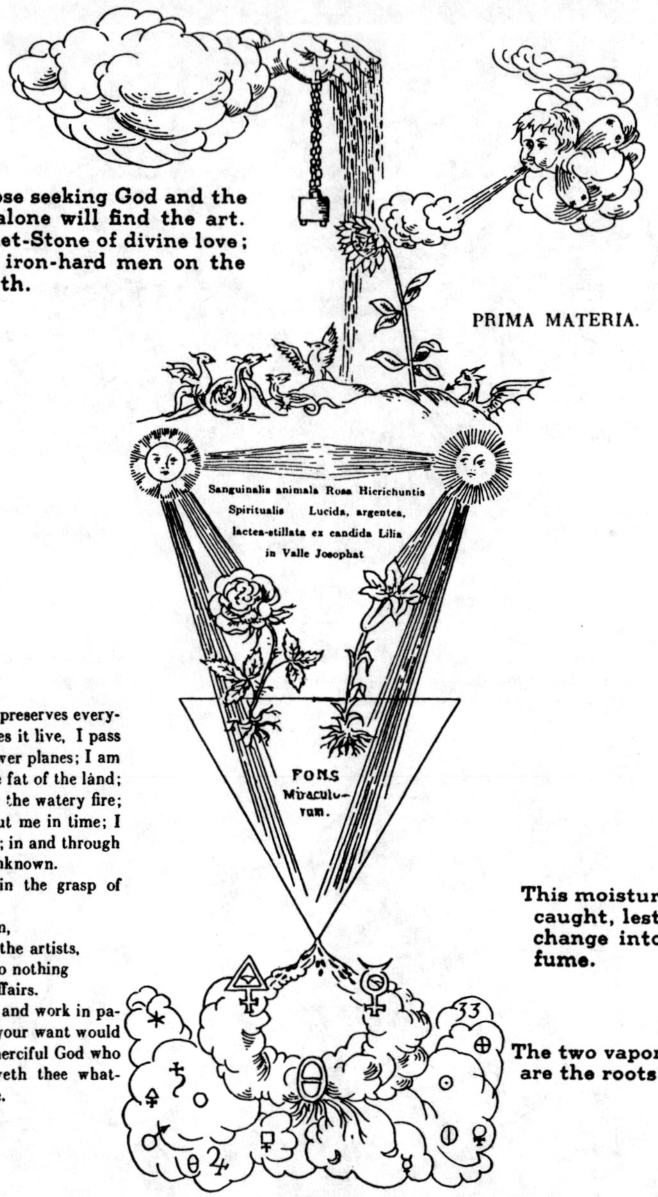

I am the moisture which preserves everything in nature and makes it live, I pass from the upper to the lower planes; I am the heavenly dew and the fat of the land; I am the fiery water and the watery fire; nothing may live without me in time; I am close to all things yea; in and through all things, nevertheless unknown.
Nevertheless I only am in the grasp of the Philosophers.
I unfold and fold up again,
Bringing contentment to the artists,
Without me thou canst do nothing
Furthering any of your affairs.
Therefore fear God, pray and work in patience, if you find me your want would cease and you have a merciful God who befriendeth thee and giveth thee whatever thy heart may desire.

This moisture must be caught, lest it should change into vapor or fume.

The two vapors or fumes are the roots of the art.

The Prima Materia derives its existence from the Fiat, the Word of creation. And this Word comes from the Father who is the creator of all things, and the Spirit radiates from both: This is God's life giving air. Then, too, air brings to life everything within the elements. The fire warms all things, the water refreshes, delights and saturates all things: And the nitrous earth, Mother-like, nourishes and sustains all things; the air was born out of fire, and in turn makes the fire burn, that it may live, but air in the form of water is food for the fire, and the fire burns into this element: Water and dew of the ground, the greasy fat dew of the ground, the earth as keeper of nitrous salt nourishes it. For the womb of the earth is the sulphuric nitrous-salt of nature, the one good thing God has created in this visible world.

The same Salt-Mother of the elements is the nitrous, aluminous and spiritual gumosic water, ⴱ earth or crystal, which has Nature in its womb, a Son of the Sun, and a Daughter of the Moon. It is a Hermaphrodite, born out of the wind, a phoenix living in fire, a pelican, reviving his dear young ones with its blood; the young Icarus, drowned in the water, whose nurse is the earth, whose Mother is the wind, whose Father is the fire, the water her caretaker and drink, one stone and no stone, one water and no water, nevertheless a stone of living power and a water of living might; a sulphur, a mercury, a salt, hidden deep in nature, and which no fool has ever known nor seen.

Deus vendit sua dona pro labore.

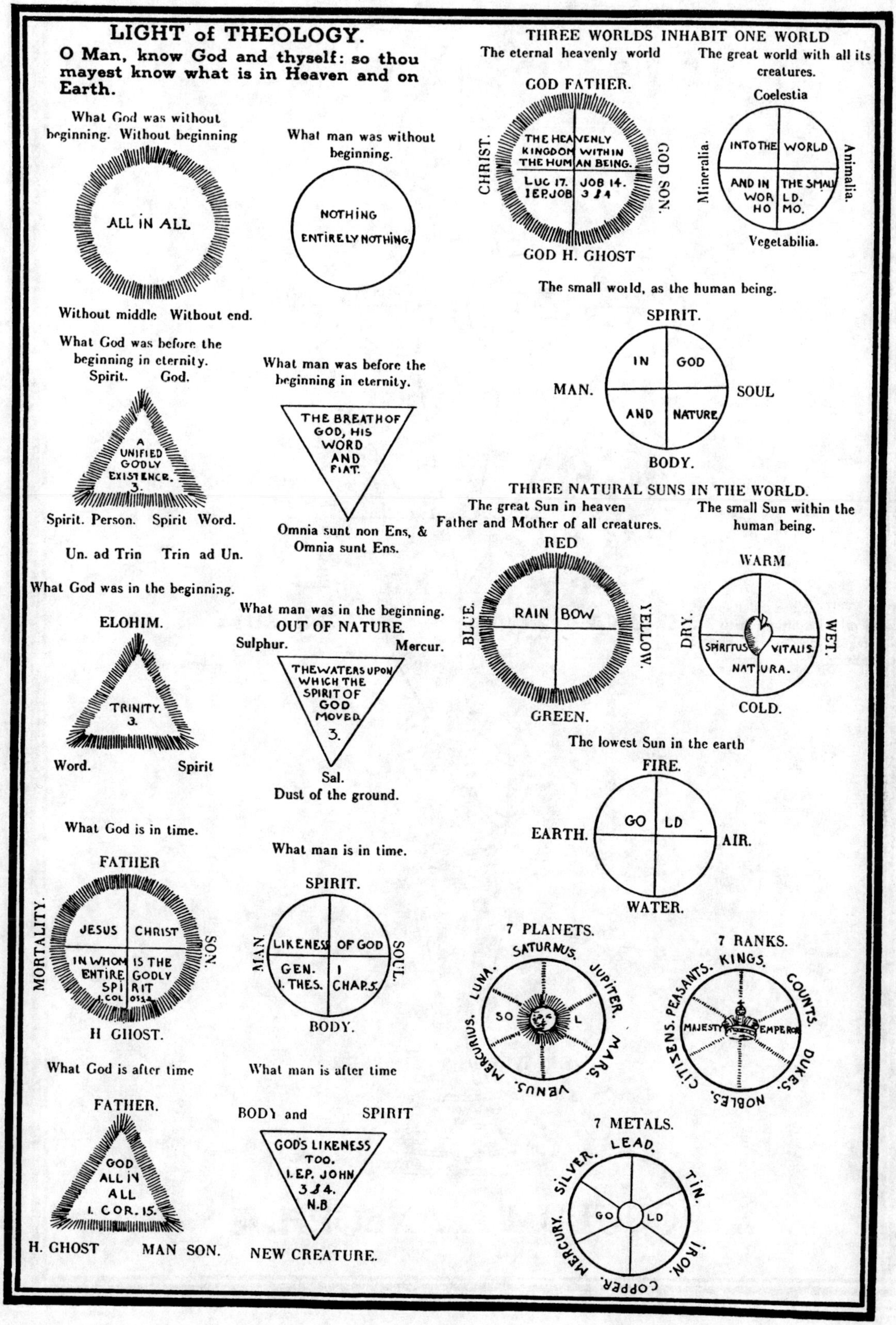

LIGHT of THEOLOGY.
O Man, know God and thyself: so thou mayest know what is in Heaven and on Earth.
What God was without beginning. Without beginning
ALL IN ALL
Without middle Without end.
What man was without beginning.
NOTHING
ENTIRELY NOTHING.
What God was before the beginning in eternity.
Spirit. God.
A UNIFIED GODLY EXISTENCE. 3.
Spirit. Person. Spirit Word.
Un. ad Trin Trin ad Un.
What man was before the beginning in eternity.
THE BREATH OF GOD, HIS WORD AND FIAT.
Omnia sunt non Ens, & Omnia sunt Ens.
What God was in the beginning.
ELOHIM.
TRINITY. 3.
Word. Spirit
What man was in the beginning.
OUT OF NATURE.
Sulphur. Mercur.
THE WATERS UPON WHICH THE SPIRIT OF GOD MOVED. 3.
Sal.
Dust of the ground.
What God is in time.
FATHER
MORTALITY.
JESUS CHRIST
IN WHOM IS THE ENTIRE GODLY SPIRIT
I. COL. 2
SON.
H GHOST.
What man is in time.
SPIRIT.
MAN.
LIKENESS OF GOD
GEN. I
I. THES. CHAP. 5.
SOUL.
BODY.
What God is after time
FATHER.
GOD ALL IN ALL
I. COR. 15.
H. GHOST MAN SON.
What man is after time
BODY and SPIRIT
GOD'S LIKENESS TOO.
I. EP. JOHN 3 & 4.
N.B
NEW CREATURE.
THREE WORLDS INHABIT ONE WORLD
The eternal heavenly world
GOD FATHER.
CHRIST.
THE HEAVENLY KINGDOM WITHIN THE HUMAN BEING.
LUC 17. JOB 14.
I EP. JOB 3 & 4
GOD SON.
GOD H. GHOST
The great world with all its creatures.
Coelestia
Mineralia.
INTO THE WORLD
AND IN THE SMALL WORLD.
HOMO.
Animalia.
Vegetabilia.
The small world, as the human being.
SPIRIT.
MAN.
IN GOD
AND NATURE
SOUL
BODY.
THREE NATURAL SUNS IN THE WORLD.
The great Sun in heaven Father and Mother of all creatures.
RED
BLUE.
RAIN BOW
YELLOW.
GREEN.
The small Sun within the human being.
WARM
DRY.
SPIRITUS VITALIS.
NATURA.
WET.
COLD.
The lowest Sun in the earth
FIRE.
EARTH.
GO LD
AIR.
WATER.
7 PLANETS.
SATURNUS.
JUPITER.
MARS.
VENUS.
MERCURIUS.
LUNA.
SOL
7 RANKS.
KINGS.
COUNTS.
DUKES.
NOBLES.
CITIZENS.
PEASANTS.
MAJESTY EMPEROR
7 METALS.
LEAD.
TIN.
IRON.
COPPER.
MERCURY.
SILVER.
GO LD

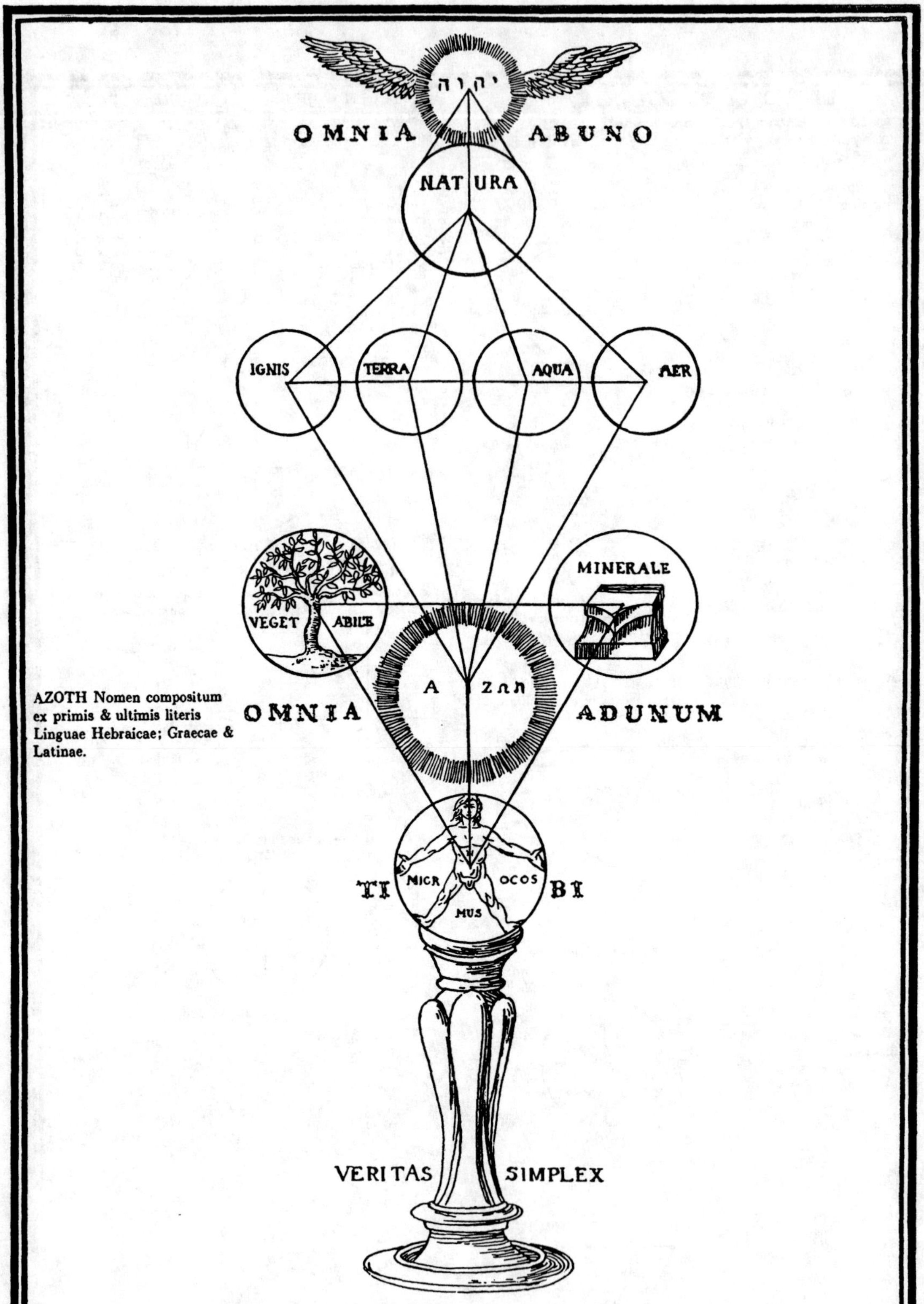

POCULUM PANSOPHIÆ.

Picture of the Human Heart in the Old and the New Creature.

GOD

This scripture must be understood out of the innermost and unto the outermost.

Everything that is in the great world, is in man too, for he is created out of it therefore he is the small world and his heart is his center Note **this well!**

God hath caused all men to be born again out of love and hath already enkindled the light within them in their Mother's womb, and He Himself, is the light, the morning star, shining from within them.

This figure explains the 1. Epistle of John, and the same explains this figure.

The starry heaven in the heart with its powers and might is subject to vanity, and time being past, then everything will be again in eternity.

A heart is wide at the top, narrow at the bottom, to be opened to God, closed to earthliness.

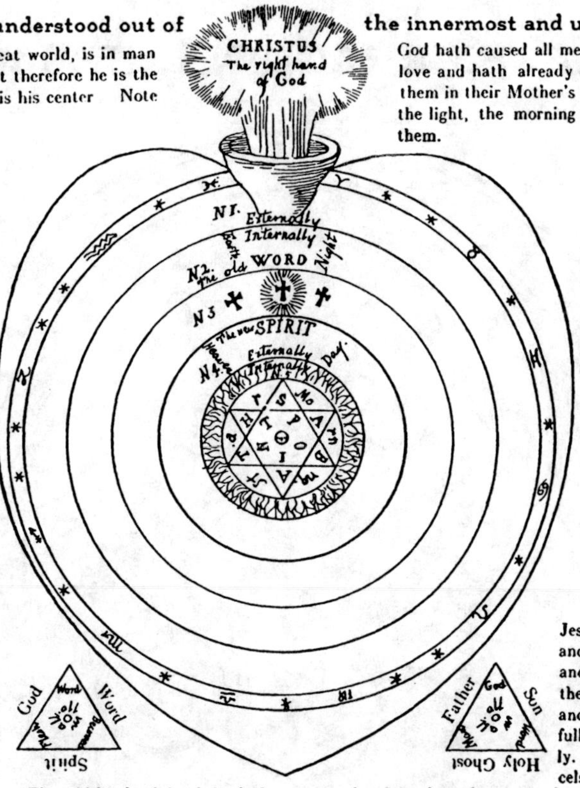

God is threefold, the Word is threefold and 2 times 3 is 6, pertaining to the innermost person and morningstar within our heart, which is Jesus Christ, the one point.

Jesus Christ yesterday, today and in eternity. Who there is and was, who there cometh, the beginning and end, Alpha and Omega, in Him is the fullness of the Godhead bodily. Hallelujah, Gloria in Excelsus Dec. Amen.

The old birth of death in darkness must be slain through cross and suffering, in a wide circle is the reason captured and through the Word, man is being led back into the spirit, into the rebirth, into the light, in Christo, where alone there is quiet, peace, eternal life and the kingdom of heaven.

No 1 Here is Christus born a man according to the flesh of Maria, about this He said in John 6. The flesh pacifieth nothing Here is the human birth from Adam, the old Creature, sinful, mortal, does not come into the heavenly kingdom, man liveth in darkness, blindness, night and death, in his reason from the power of the stars and the 4 Elements, out of which come sickness, out of which are invented the handling of the arts, higher schools, ecclesiastical and secular offices and position, so far they are in the heart Over which rules the authority which God ordered All this is in vain and mortal, into this darkness shineth the light and the darkness comprehendeth it not Herein belong Christians, Jews, Turks and heathens, they are altogether sinners and lack the glory they ought to have before God; they are all resolved in God's wrath

No 2. Here Christus is grieved in his soul and tempted by the devil, the innermost conscience out of the stars is being tempted by lust of the eyes, deed of the flesh and of vanity, with assurance and despair. Here the Holy Scriptures become dead letters, bringing forth sects, superstitious and fleshly priests, fearing God's word might be taken away from them, meaning the dead letter The authorities want to fight with the sword for religion, killing the believers, Christ and His apostles, thinking to serve God, divine things are just so much foolishness to them, they can understand Christ only in the flesh and according to the tribe of David, they make divisions, cliques, and sects.

No 3. Here is the separation of light from darkness, the dawn comes up, all temporalites will be foresaken, through many sorrows we have to enter into the kingdom of God, man is a fool to the world, Christ is being crucified in him and he in Christ, therefore he is a cross to the world and the world a cross to him, here stands calmness, whoever turneth toward the light lives in Christ and Christ in him in time and eternity.

No. 4 The old hath to go entirely: for behold: I make all things new Here is the rebirth by water and spirit, from on high through the word of truth, a new creature born of God Christ hath become flesh, ressurected in the human being, awakening him from the dead, nourishing him with his real flesh and blood unto life. Christ is the word of the father, the book of life, the Gospel, the power of God He causeth belief, and He blesseth He is king, ruling with the sword of the spirit, man becometh divine nature, hath his life in heaven with Christ.

No. 5 The Holy Ghost is the ointment, teacheth men innermost Divine things; man hath become a temple of God, indwelt by the Holy Trinity Christ in man, God and man, cringing about love Christus is all in all, the sole One.

O LORD, merciful GOD, open the human heart, to understand Thy secrets through the Holy Ghost.

Who hath well understood the figure,
Hath understanding, also, of the scriptures.
Three worlds hath God created,
In heaven love, on earth mercy,
Wrath in hell and darkness;
This certainly is a picture of man.
On this earth he only hath to choose
Which way to go, the end is to his will.

TABULA SMARAGDINA HERMETIS.

VERBA SECRETORUM HERMETIS.

It is true, certain, and without falsehood, that whatever is below is like that which is above; and that which is above is like that which is below: to accomplish the one wonderful work. As all things are derived from the One Only Thing, by the will and by the word of the One Only One who created it in His Mind, so all things owe their existence to this Unity by the order of Nature, and can be improved by Adaptation to that Mind.

Its Father is the Sun; its Mother is the Moon; the Wind carries it in its womb; and its nurse is the Earth. This Thing is the Father of all perfect things in the world. Its power is most perfect when it has again been changed into Earth Separate the Earth from the Fire, the subtle from the gross, but carefully and with great judgment and skill.

It ascends from earth to heaven, and descends again, new born, to the earth, taking unto itself thereby the power of the Above and the Below. Thus the splendor of the whole world will be thine, and all darkness shall flee from thee.

This is the strongest of all powers, the Force of all forces, for it overcometh all subtle things and can penetrate all that is solid For thus was the world created, and rare combinations, and wonders of many kinds are wrought

Hence I am called HERMES TRISMEGISTUS, having mastered the three parts of the wisdom of the whole world. What I have to say about the masterpiece of the alchemical art, the Solar Work, is now ended.

INTERPRETATION and EXPLANATION of the
TABULA SMARAGDINA HERMEDIS

This picture, plain and insignificant in appearance,
  Concealeth a great and important thing.
Yea, it containeth a secret of the kind
  That is the greatest treasure in the world.
For what on this earth is deemed more excellent
  Than to be a Lord who ever recketh with gold,
And hath also a healthy body,
  Fresh and hale all his life long,
Until the predestined time
  That cannot be overstepped by any creature.
All this, as I have stated, clearly
  Is contained within this figure.
Three separate shields are to be seen,
  And on them are eagle, lion, and free star.
And painted in their very midst
  Artfully stands an imperial globe.
Heaven and Earth in like manner
  Are also placed herein intentionally,
And between the hands outstretched towards each other
  Are to be seen the symbols of metals.
And in the circle surrounding the picture
  Seven words are to be found inscribed.
Therefore I shall now tell
  What each meaneth particularly
And then indicate without hesitation
  How it is called by name.
Therein is a secret thing of the Wise
  In which is to be found great power.
And how to prepare it will also
  Be described in the following:
The three shields together indicate
  Sal, *Sulphur*, and *Mercurium*.
The *Sal* hath been one *Corpus* that
  Is the very last one in the Art.
The *Sulphur* henceforth is the soul
  Without which the body can do nothing.
Mercurius is the spirit of power,
  Holding together both body and soul,
Therefore it is called a medium
  Since whatever is made without it hath no stability.
For soul and body could not die
  Should spirit also be with them.
And soul and spirit could not be
  Unless they had a body to dwell in,
And no power had body or spirit
  If the soul did not accompany them.
This is the meaning of the Art:
  The body giveth form and constancy,
The soul doth dye and tinge it,
  The spirit maketh it fluid and penetrateth it.
And therefore the Art cannot be
  In one of these three things alone.
Nor can the greatest secret exist alone:
  It must have body, soul, and spirit.
And now what is the fourth,
  From which the three originate,
The same names teach thee
  And the sevenfold star in the lower shield.
The Lion likewise by its colour and power
  Showeth its nature and its property.
In the Eagle yellow and white are manifest.
  Mark my words well, for there is need of care:
The imperial orb doth exhibit
  The symbol of this highest good.

Heaven and earth, four elements,
  Fire, light, and water, are therein.
The two hands do testify with an oath
  The right reason and the true knowledge,
And from what roots are derived
  All of the metals and many other things.
Now there remain only the seven words,
  Hear further what they mean:
If thou dost now understand this well
  This knowledge shall nevermore fail thee.
Every word standeth for a city
  Each of which hath but one gate.
☉ The first signifieth gold, is intentionally yellow.
☽ The second for fair white silver.
☿ The third, *Mercurius*, is likewise grey.
♃ The fourth for tin, is heaven-blue.
♂ The fifth for iron, is blood-red.
♀ The sixth for copper, is true green.
♄ The seventh for lead, is black as coal.
  Mark what I mean, understand me well:
In these city gates, indeed,
  Standeth the whole ground of the Art.
For no one city alone can effect anything,
  The others must also be close at hand.
And as soon as the gates are closed
  One cannot enter any city.
And if they had no gates
  Not one thing could they accomplish.
But if these gates are close together
  A ray of light appeareth from seven colors.
Shining very brightly together
  Their might is incomparable.
Thou canst not find such wonders on earth,
  Wherefore hearken unto further particulars:
Seven letters, and seven words,
  Seven cities, and seven gates,
Seven times, and seven metals,
  Seven days, and seven ciphers.
Whereby I mean seven herbs
  Also seven arts and seven stones.
Therein stands every lasting art.
  Well for him who findeth this.
If this be too hard for thee to understand
  Here me again in a few other particulars:
Truly I reveal to thee
  Very clearly and plainly, without hatred or envy,
How it is named with one word
  Vitriol, for him who understandeth it.
If thou wouldst oft figure out
  This Cabbalistic way with all diligence,
Seven and fifty in the cipher
  Thou findest figured everywhere.
Let not the Work discourage thee,
  Understand me rightly, so shalt thou enjoy it.
Besides that, note this fully,
  There is a water which doth not make wet.
From it the metals are produced,
  It is frozen as hard as ice.
A moistened dust a fuller wind doth raise,
  Wherein are all qualities.
If thou dost not understand this,
  Then I may not name it for thee otherwise.
Now I will instruct thee
  How it should be prepared.

There are seven ways for this art,
  If thou neglectest any of them thou workest in vain.
But thou must, before all things else, know
  Thou hast to succeed in purification.
And although this be twofold,
  Thou art in need of one alone.
The first work is freely done by it
  Without any other addition,
Without distilling something in it,
  Simply through its putrefication.
From all of its earthliness
  Is everything afterwards prepared.
This first way hath two paths,
  Happy is he who goeth on the right path.
The first extendeth through the strength of fire,
  With and in itself, note this well.
The second extendeth further
  Until one cometh to treasure and to gain.
This is done by dissolving,
  And again by saturating, I inform you:
This must be undertaken first of all,
  So comest thou to the end of the fine art.
After the whole purification hath been completed
  It will be prepared and boiled in the sun
Or in the warm dung of its time,
  Which extendeth itself very far
Until it becometh constant and perfect,
  And the treasure of the Wise is in it.
The other ways are very subtle
  And many mighty one fail therein,
For here is the purpose of the distillation
  And the sublimation of the Wise Men.
The separation of the four elements
  Is also called by the Wise Men
Air, water, and rectified fire.
  The earth on the ground hath mislead many,
Having been deemed a worthless thing,
  Although all the power lieth in it.
Some know not how to separate it
  From their *Cortibus*, therefore they fail.
It was cast behind the door,
  But the Wise Man taketh it up again,
Purifieth it snow-white and clear:
  This is the ground, I say in truth.
But if thou dost wish to separate it,
  Note that it is of no little importance,
For if they are not prepared
  Then you are in error, that I swear.
Therefore thou must also have some vinegar
  Which is revealed to the Wise Men,
Wherewith thou wilt effect the separation,
  So that nothing earthly remaineth in it any more,
Till body and soul have to be separated,
  Otherwise called fire and earth
And after they are thus purified,

☛ ☛ ☛

And thereupon followeth the mixture, observe!
  And so it cometh to a wondrous strength,
The finished figures with the unfinished.
  And if the fire be likewise rightly controlled,
It will be entirely perfect
  In much less time than a year.
Now thou hast the entire way in its length
  On which are not more than two paths.
From these one soon wandereth and goeth astray,
  Else it all standeth clear and plain.
The one is the water of the Wise Men,
  Which is the *Mercurius* alone.
The other is called a vinegar,
  And it is known only to a very few.
And this vinegar doth circle
  Away from the philosophical iron.
It is Lord *Aes* whom it maketh glad.
  Therefore they have combined so closely
Many hundred forms and names are given
  After each hath chosen it.
One way springeth from the true source,
  A few have worked on it for a whole year.
But many through their art and craft
  Have shortened so long a space of time.
And quickly is the preparation set free
  As Alchemy doth point out.
The preparation alone
  Maketh this stone great and glorious.
Although there is but one matter
  It lacketh nothing else.
But when it is clarified
  Its name hath misled many.
However, I have revealed enough to thee
  In many ways, forms, and fashions.
There are many names; I say
  Let not thyself be misled from the true way.
In their scriptures the Elders write
  That it is a draught, a great poison.
Others call it a snake, a monster,
  Which is not costly anywhere.
It is common to all men
  Throughout the world, to rich and also to poor.
It is the property of the metals
  Through which they conquer victoriously.
The same is a perfection
  And setteth a golden crown upon it.
Now the practice is completed
  For him who understandeth it and knoweth the matter.
Only two things more are to be chosen
  Which thou wilt find by now
If thou dost follow the right way
  And attend carefully to thy work.
The composition is the one
  Which the Wise Men kept secret.
The nature of the fire also hath hidden craft;
  Therefore its order is another.
With that, one should, not deal too much
  Or else all execution is lost.
One cannot be too subtle with it.
  As the hen hatcheth out the chick
So also shall it be in the beginning,
  And time itself will prove it.
For just as the fire is regulated
  Will this treasure itself be produced.
Be industrious, constant, peaceful, and pious,
  And also ask God for His help:
If thou dost obtain that, then always remember
  The poor and their needs.

AUREUM SECULUM REDIVIVUM

That is

The Very Ancient Golden Age Having Passed Away

Which now hath risen again, blossomed in loveliness, and produced fragrant golden seed
This precious and noble seed is pointed out and revealed to all true *Sapientiae and doctrinae filiis* by
HENRICUS MADATHANUS, THEOSOPHUS,
Medicus and tandem, Dei gratia aureae crucis frater.

Epistle of James, i:5:
If any of you lack wisdom, let him ask of God that giveth to all men liberally and upraideth not; and it shall be given him.

SYMBOLUM AUTHORIS
Centrum mundi, granum fundi

FOREWORD

To the Christian and Worthy Reader

Kind and God-loving Reader, and especially you sapientiae and doctrinae filii, some years ago Almighty God opened mine eyes with the enlightenment of His Holy Spirit (from Whom we receive all wisdom and Who was sent unto us through Christ from the Father), because I had prayed fervently, unceasingly, and constantly and had called upon Him many times So that I beheld the true *Centrum in Trigono centri* the one and true *substance* of the Noble Philosopher's Stone, and although I had it in mine own hands for the length of five years, I did not know how to use it profitably, rightly, or befittingly, how to extract from it the *red lion's blood* and the *white eagle's gluten*, much less how to mix, enclose, and seal it according to the proportionate weight of Nature, or how to commit it to and proceed with the hidden fire, all of which must be done not without understanding and care. And although I searched in the *scriptis, parabolis and variis Philosophorum figuris* with special care and understanding, and laboured diligently to solve their manifold strange *aenigmata*, which existed in part only in their own minds, I found out *reipsa* that this was sheer phantasy and nonsense, as also testify the *Aurora Philosophorum*. They are all foolishness, like all the *praeparationes*, even of *Geber* and *Albertus Magnus*, with their *purgationes, sublimationes, cementationes, distillationes, rectificationes, circulationes, putrefactiones, conjunctiones, solutiones, assensiones, coagulationes, calcinationes, incinerationes, mortificationes, revificationes*, etc. In like manner are their tripods, *Alanthor*, reflecting ovens, smelting furnaces, putrescences, horse-dung, ashes, sand, cupping-glasses, pelican vials, retorts, fixatoriums, etc., sophistical, futile, and useless things. Personally, I have in truth to admit this: especially since noble Nature, which letteth itself be easily found in its own innate *substance*, doth not know of any of these things. There are those who look for the *materiam lapidis* in wine, in the imperfect body, in blood, in marcasite, in mercury, in sulphur, in urine, in stercorate, in auripigment, and in herbs such as chelidonium, lungwort, yew, hyssop, etc. Theophrastus, in his *Secreto Magico de Lapide Philosophorum*, rightly says of them: all this is villainy and thievery, with which they mislead other people, take their money, spend and waste their time uselessly and vainly, follow only their own fool's-head, but who cannot figure out in advance the requirements of Nature. Rather tell me one thing: What dost thou think of those who burn water in the mines of the Earth, or are there also people therein who enhance the value of wine, or burn the urine of small children to make metals therewith? Or dost thou think there is any apothecary therein who hath for sale any thing with which thou canst make metals? Thou fool, canst thou not understand that thou dost err, that none of these things belong to Nature? Or dost thou want to be above God, that thou dost want to make metals out of blood? Thou mightest as well try to make a man out of a horse, or a cow out of a mouse, to give good milk in addition This, too, would be a multiplication, but these things do not happen, and as little as they can happen, so little canst thou make metals with the above-mentioned recipes, for this is not a Nature-given art And whatever Nature hath made, no art can effect; for if a woman hath given birth to a boy, no art can change the boy into a girl, whatever means might be employed for that purpose. After this short discourse, it should be easy for anyone to see how, and in what form, the *materia benedicta* should be sought and found. And no one should imagine, much less be persuaded by any clowns, that he really hath in his hands the *veram materiam* either through the secret revelation of God or through those who claim to be acquainted with it, and no one should imagine that he would then be able to disintegrate the said *veram materiam* proportionately, to separate the *purum ab impuro* in the highest things, that he knoweth how to purify it and completely understandeth. Nay, my dear analysts, that is by no means so: therein lies the difficulty, and to such matters belong art and a skilled mind. See me, for example: as you heard from me in the beginning, for five years I was acquainted with the *veram materiam lapidis*, but all that time I did not know how to proceed with it, and not until the sixth year was the key to its power entrusted to me through the secret revelation of Almighty God. And the old Patriarchs, Prophets, and *Philosophi* have at all times kept this key hidden and secret, for the *Monarcha in loco dicto* saith: It would be a great theft, and no longer secret, had they revealed it in their writings, so that every cobbler and tooth-drawer could understand it, and much evil could be done that way which would be against the will of the Lord, etc. Now there are many reasons why I should write this Tract: some are mentioned here, some in the *Epilogo*, and another reason is that I do not want to appear as if I would have for my exclusive use *talentum a Deo mihi commissum* (a talent intrusted to me by God). So I have written down in this, my *Aureo seculo redivivo* (*Golden Age Restored*), as much as God and Nature have permitted me, about the great secret of the Philosophers, as mine eyes have witnessed it and my hands grasped it, and how it was revealed through the mercy of God at the right time in great might and glory: and may the pious and God-loving reader take all this in good faith and accept it, examine it skillfully, and be not perturbed if at times there are words mixed up with my sayings which seem to be contrary to the letter. I could not write otherwise *per Theoriam ad praxim*, because it is forbidden to write more exactly and clearly about this *in republica chymica*. But undoubtedly all those who read this Tract in true confidence with the inner eyes of their minds, and are able to look upon it in the right way, to study it diligently, and who pray in all things inwardly and with all their heart, will enjoy, as I did, the wondrously sweet philosophical fruit hidden therein, and partake of it, according to God's will. And then they will be and will remain true Brothers of the Golden Cross, and in eternal alliance, chosen members of the Philosophical Community.

Finally, I will be so candid as to disclose my true given and family name in the following manner to the intelligent, worthy, and Christian reader, so that no one will have a right to cry out against me. So now let it be known to everyone that the number of my name is M.DCXII, in which number my full name was inscribed in the book of Nature by 11 dead and 7 living. Moreover, the letter 5 is the fifth part of the 8, and the 15 is again the fifth part of the 12, and let this suffice thee.

Datum in Monte Abiegno, die 25. Martii Anno 1621

EPIGRAMMA

ad Sapientiae and doctrinae filios.

Quae sivi: inveni: purgavi saepius: atque
Conjunxi: maturavi: Tinctura secuta est
Aurea. Naturae centrum quae dicitur: inde
Tot sensus, tot scripta virum, variaeque figurae
Omnibus, ingenue fateor, MEDICINA metallis;
Infirmisque simul: punctum divinitus ortum.

HARMANNUS DATICHIUS:,
Auth famulus.

What I have eagerly desired, I have found: I have purified more often: and
I have united: I have brought to maturity: the resulting Tincture is
Golden, which is called the centre of Nature: thence
So many sensations, so many writings of men, and manifold forms.
In all, I frankly admit, the MEDICINA in metals;
And in the feeble as well: the point risen from heaven.

AUREUM SECULUM

REDIVIUM. (*The Golden Age Restored*).

Whilst I was meditating upon the wonders of the Most High and the secrets of hidden Nature and the fiery and fervent love of the neighbor, I recalled the white harvest where Reuben, the son of Leah, had found in the fields and had given the mandrakes Rachel had gotten from Leah for sleeping with the patriarch Jacob. But my thoughts went much deeper and led me further to Moses, how he had made a *potable* of the solar-calf cast by Aaron, and how he had it burned with fire, ground to powder, strewed it upon the waters, and gave it to the Children of Israel to drink. And I marvelled most about this prompt and ingenius destruction which the hand of God had wrought But after pondering over it for some time my eyes were opened, just as happened with the two disciples at Emmaus who knew the Lord in the Breaking of Bread, and my heart burned within me. But I laid down and began to sleep And, lo, in my dream King Solomon appeared to me, in all his might, wealth, and glory, leading beside him all the women of his harem: there were threescore queens, and fourscore concubines, and virgins without number, but one was his gentle dove, most beautiful and dearest to his heart, and according to Catholic custom she held a magnificent procession wherein the *Centrum* was highly honored and cherished, and its name was like an out-ointment, the fragrance of which surpassed all spices. And its fiery spirit was a key to open the temple, to enter the Holy Place, and to grasp the horns of the altar.

When the procession was ended, Solomon showed unto me the unified *Centrum in Itrigoni centri* and opened my understanding to me, and I became aware that behind me stood a nude woman with a bloody wound in her breast, out of which came forth blood and water, but the joints of her thighs were like jewels, the work of the hands of a cunning workman, her navel was like a round goblet, which wanteth not liquor, her belly was like an heap of wheat set about with roses, her two breasts were like two young roses that are twins, her neck was as a tower of ivory, her eyes like the fishpools in Heshbon by the gate of Bath-rabbim: her nose was as the tower of Lebanon which looketh towards Damascus. Her head was like Carmel, and the hair of her head was tied in many folds, like king's purple. But her garments, which she threw off, lay at her feet, and were all unsightly, stinking, and poisonous And she began to speak: I have put off my coat, how shall I put it on? I have washed my feet, how shall I defile them? The watchmen that went about the city found me, they smote me, they wounded me, and took away my veil from me. Then was I stricken with fear and not conscious and fell upon the ground: but Solomon bade me stand up again and said: be not afraid when thou dost see Nature bare, and the most hidden which is beneath heaven and upon the earth. She is beautiful as Tirzah, comely as Jerusalem, terrible as an army with banners, but nevertheless she is the pure chaste virgin out of whom Adam was made and created Sealed and hidden is the entrance to her house, for she dwelleth in the garden and sleepeth in the twofold caves of Abraham on the field Ephron, and her palace is the depths of the Red Sea, and in the deep transparent chasms, the air hath given her birth and the fire hath brought her up, wherefore she is a queen of the country, milk and honey hath she in her breasts. Yea, her lips are like a dripping honey-comb, honey and milk are under her tongue and the smell of her garments is like the fragrance of Lebanon to the Wise, but an abomination to the ignorant. And Solomon said further: Rouse thee, look upon all my women and see if you can find her equal. And forthwith the woman had to cast off her garments and I looked at her, but my mind had lost the power of judgment, and mine eyes were holden, so that I did not recognise her.

But as Solomon observed my weakness, he separated his women from this nude woman and said: Thy thoughts are vain and the sun hath burned out thy mind and thy memory is as black as fog, so thou canst not judge aright, so if thou wouldst not forfeit thy concern and take advantage of the present opportunity, then can the bloody sweat and snow-white tears of this nude virgin again refresh thee, cleanse thine understanding and memory and restore it fully, so that thine eyes may perceive the wonders of the Most High, the height of the uppermost, and thou shalt really fathom the foundations of all Nature, the power and operation of all the Elements, and thine understanding will be as fine silver, and thy memory as gold, the colors of all precious stones will appear before thine eyes and thou wilt know their production, and thou wilt know how to separate good from evil, the goats from the sheep. Thy life will be very peaceful, but the cymbals of Aaron will awaken thee from sleep and the harp of David, my father, from thy slumber. After Solomon thus spake, I was very much more afraid, and was exceedingly terrified, partly because of his heartbreaking works, also partly because of the great glamor and splendor of the present queenly woman, and Solomon took me by the hand and led me through a wine cellar into a secret but very stately hall, where he refreshed me with flowers and apples, but its windows were made out of transparent crystals and I looked through them And he said: What dost thou see? I replied: I can only see from this hall into the hall I just left, and on the left standeth thy queenly woman, and on the right the nude virgin, and her eyes are redder than wine, her teeth whiter than milk, but her garments at her feet are more unsightly, blacker, and more filthy than the brook of Kidron From all of them choose one, said Solomon to be thy beloved I esteem her and my queen alike and highly, pleased as I am with the loveliness of my wives, so little do I care about the abomination of her garments And as soon as the king had thus spoken, he turned around and conversed in a very friendly way with one of his queens. Amongst these was an hundred-year-old stewardess, with a grey cloak, a black cap upon her head, bedecked wih numberless snow-white pearls and lined with red velvet, and embroidered and sewn in an artful manner with blue and yellow silk, and her cloak was adorned with divers Turkish colors and Indian figures: this old woman beckoned to me secretly and swore unto me an holy oath that she was the mother of the nude virgin, that she had been born from her body, and that she was a chaste, pure and secluded virgin, that until now she had not suffered any man to look upon her, and although she had let herself be used everywhere among the many people on the streets, no one had ever seen her naked before now, and no one had touched her, for she was the virgin of whom the Prophet said: Behold, we have a son born unto us in secret, who is transformed beside others; behold, the virgin had brought forth, such a virgin as is called *Apdorossa*, meaning: secretly, she who cannot suffer others. But while this her daughter was as yet unwed, she had her marriage-portion lying under her feet, because of the present danger of the war, so that she would be robbed of it by some roving soldiery and denuded of her stately treasure. However I should not be frightened because of her disgusting garments, but choose her daughter before all others for the delight of my love and life. Then she would give and reveal to me a lye to clean her garments, and then I would obtain a liquid salt and non-combustible oil for my house-keeping, and an immeasurable treasure, and her right hand would always caress me and her left hand would be under my head And as I then wanted to declare myself categorically upon this matter, Solomon turned around again, looked upon me, and said: I am the wisest man on earth, beautiful and pleasing are my wives and the glamor of my queens surpasseth the gold of Ophir; the adornments of my concubines overshadow the rays of the sun, and the beauty of my virgins surpasseth the rays of the moon, and as heavenly as are my women, my wisdom is unfathomable and my knowledge is inexplicable. Whereupon I answered and, half afraid, I bowed: Lo, I have found grace in thine eyes, and since I am poor, give me this nude virgin. I choose her amongst all others for the duration of my life, and though her garments are filthy and torn, I will clean them and love her with all mine heart, and she shall be my sister, my bride, because she hath ravished mine heart with one of her eyes, with one chain of her neck When I had thus spoken, Solomon gave her unto me, and there was a great commotion in the hall of his women, so that I was awakened by it, and I knew not what had happened to me, nevertheless I believed it to be but a dream and I thought many subtle thoughts about my dream until the morning. But after I had arisen and said my prayers, Lo! I saw the garments of the nude virgin before my bed, but no trace of her. And I began to be greatly afraid and all my hair stood upright upon my head and my whole body was bathed in cold sweat; but I took heart, recalling my dream, and thought about it again in the fear of the Lord. But my thoughts did not explain it, and for this reason I dared not to scrutinize the garments, much less to recognize anything in them I then changed my sleeping-chamber and I left the garments in it for some length of time *ex mera tamen ignorantia*, in the belief that if I were to touch them or turn them over, something peculiar would happen to me, but in my sleep the smell of the garments had poisoned and inflamed me violently, so that mine eyes could not see the time of mercy, and never

could mine heart recognise the great wisdom of Solomon.

After the above-mentioned garments had lain for five years in my sleeping-chamber and I knew not what they were good for, I finally thought to burn them, in order to clean up the place And then I spent the whole day going around with such thoughts. But the next night there appeared to me in my dream the hundred-year-old woman and she spake harshly to me thus: Thou ungrateful man: for five years I have entrusted to thee my daughter's garments; among them are her most precious jewels, and during all that time thou hast neither cleaned them nor thrown out of them the moths and worms, and now, finally, thou dost want to burn these clothes, and is it not enough that thou art the reason for the death and perishing of my daughter? Whereupon I became hot-headed and answered her: How shall I understand thee, that thou wouldst make a murderer of me? For five years mine eyes have not beheld thy daughter, and not the least did I hear of her, how then can I be the cause of her death? But she would not let me finish, and said: It is all true, but thou hast sinned against God, therefore thou couldst not obtain my daughter, nor the philosophical lixivium I promised thee for washing and cleaning her garments: for in the beginning, when Solomon willingly gave thee my daughter, and when thou didst abhor her garments, that made furious the Planet Saturn, who is her grandfather, and full of wrath was he that he transformed her again into what she had been before her birth; and since you infuriated Saturnus through thine abhorring, thou didst cause her death, putrefaction, and her final destruction, for she is the one of whom *Senior* saith: Ah, woe! to bring a nude woman unto me, when my first body was not good to look upon, and I had never been mother until I was born again, then I brought forth the power of all roots of herbs, and in mine innermost being I was victorious Such and similar heart-breaking words were very strange to me, but nevertheless I withheld mine indignation as much as was humanly possible for me, at the same time protesting *solemniter* against her sayings: that I knew nothing at all about her daughter, much less about her death and putrefaction, and although I kept her garments for five years in my sleeping-chamber, I did not know them for my great blindness nor ever discovered their use, and therefore I was innocent before God and all others This, my righteous and well-founded excuse, must have pleased the old woman not a little, for she looked at me and said: I feel and observe from thy righteous mind, that thou art innocent, and thine innocence shall be rewarded well and plentifully, therefore I will reveal to thee secretly and out of my good heart, namely that my daughter, out of special love and affection towards thee, hath left thee a gray marbled casket as an inheritance amongst her garments, which is covered with a rough, black, dirty case (and meanwhile she gave me a glass filled with lye, and continued speaking), this same little casket thou shalt clean from its stench and dirt which it hath received from the garments Thou hast no need of a key, but it will open itself, and thou wilt find two things therein: a white silver box, filled with magnificent ground-lead and polished diamonds, and another golden work of art, adorned with costly solar rubies: and this is the treasure and entire legacy of my deceased daughter which she left for thee to inherit before her transformation. If thou wilt only transfer this treasure and purify it most highly and silently and lock it up with great patience in a warm, hidden, steamy, transparent and moist cellar, and protect it from freezing, hail, quick lightning, hot thunder, and other outward destruction till the wheat harvest, then thou wilt first perceive the entire glory of thine inheritance and take part of it. Meanwhile I awoke for a second time and called upon God, full of fear, praying that He would open mine understanding that I might seek for the casket which was promised me in my dream And after my prayer was ended I sought with greatest diligence in the garments and found the casket, but the casing was tight around it and seemed grown onto it by nature, so that I was not able to take it off; then I could not clean it with any lye nor split it with iron, steel, or any other metal. I left it alone once more and did not know what to do with it, and held it to be witchcraft, thinking of the prophet's saying: For though thou wash thee with lye, and take thee much soap, yet thine iniquity is marked before me, saith the Lord God.

And after a year had passed again and I did not know, after speculating and industriously deliberating, how to remove the casing, I finally went to walk in the garden to rid myself of the melancholy thoughts, and after long promenading, I sat down on a flinty stone and fell into a deep sleep. I slept, but my heart was awake: there appeared unto me the hundred-year-old stewardess and said: Hast thou received my daughter's inheritance? In a sad voice I answered no, though I found the casket, but alone it is still impossible for me to separate the casing therefrom, and the lye thou hast given me will not work on the casing. After this simple speech the old woman smiled and said: Dost thou want to eat shells and shellfish with the shells? Do they not have to be brought forth and prepared by the very old planet and cook *Vulcan?* I told thee to clean the gray casket thoroughly with the lye given thee, and which proceeded wholly from it, and was not refined from the outer rough casing This thou hast especially to burn in the fire of the philosophers, then everything will turn out for the best. And thereupon she gave me several glowing coals wrapped up in white light taffeta and instructed me further and pointed out that I should make therefrom a philosophical and quite artful fire and burn the casing, then I would soon find the gray casket. And presently every hour a north and south wind rose, both sweeping at the same time through the garden, whereupon I awoke, rubbed the sleep out of mine eyes, and noticed that the glowing coals wrapped in white taffeta lay at my feet; with haste and joy I grasped them, prayed diligently, called upon God, studied and labored day and night, and thought meanwhile of the great and excellent sayings of the *Philosophers*, who say: *Ignis et azoth tibi sufficiunt.* About this *Esdras* saith in his fourth book: And he gave unto me a full cup which was full of fire, and his form was as of fire, and when I had drunk of it, my heart uttered understanding, and wisdom grew in my breast, for my spirit retained its memory: and my mouth was opened, and shut no more The Most High gave understanding unto the five men, and they wrote by course the things that were told them, in characters which they knew not So in forty days were written 204 books, 70 for the wisest alone, who were truly worthy of it, and all were written on box-wood And then I proceeded *in silentio et spe*, as the old woman had revealed to me in my dream until, according to Solomon's prediction, after a long time my knowledge became silver and my memory became golden. But according to the instructions and teaching of the old stewardess, I enclosed and locked up in a proper and quite artistic manner the treasure of her daughter, namely: the splendid and brilliant lunar diamonds and the solar rubies, both of which came forth and were found from the casket and the landscape. I heard the voice of Solomon who said: My beloved is white and ruddy, the chiefest among ten thousand. His head is as the most fine gold, his locks are bushy, and black as a raven. His eyes are as the eyes of doves by the rivers of waters, washed with milk, and fitly set His cheeks are as a bed of spices, as sweet flowers: his lips are like roses, dropping sweet smelling myrrh His hands are as gold rings set with the beryl: his belly is as bright ivory overlaid with sapphires. His legs are as pillars of marble, set upon sockets of fine gold: his countenance is as Lebanon, excellent as the cedars. His mouth is most sweet: yea, he is altogether lovely. This is my beloved, and this is my friend, O daughters of Jerusalem. Therefore shalt thou hold him, and not let him go, until thou bringest him into his mother's house, and into his mother's chamber. And when Solomon had spoken these words I knew not how to answer him, and I became silent, but I wanted nevertheless to open up again the locked-up treasure, with which I might remain unmolested Then I heard another voice: I charge you, O ye daughters of Jerusalem, by the roes, and by the hinds of the field, that ye stir not up, nor awake my love, till she please, for she is a garden inclosed, a spring shut up, a fountain sealed, the vineyard at Baal-hamon, the vineyard at Engeddi, the garden of fruits and spices, the mountain of myrrh, the hill of frankincense, the bed, the litter, the crown, the palm-tree and apple-tree, the flower of Sharon, the sapphire, the turquoise, the wall, tower, and rampart, the garden of joy, the well in the garden, the spring of living water, the king's daughter, and the love of Solomon in his concupiscence: she is the dearest to her mother, and the chosen of her mother, but her head is filled with dew, and her locks with the drops of the night

Through this discourse and revelation I was so far informed that I knew the purpose of the Wise and did not touch the locked treasure until through God's mercy, the working of noble Nature, and the work of mine own hands, the work was happily completed

Shortly after this time, just on the day of the month when the moon was new, there occurred an eclipse of the sun, showing itself in all its terrifying power, in the beginning dark green and some mixed colors, until it finally became coal-black, darkened heaven and earth, and many people were much afraid, but I rejoiced, thinking of God's great mercy, and the new birth, as Christ Himself pointed out to us, that a grain of wheat must be cast into the ground, that it may not rot therein, else it bringeth forth no fruit And then it happened that the darkness was covered with clouds, and the sun began to shine through, yet at the same time three parts of it were still heavily darkened; and lo, an arm broke through the clouds, and my body trembled because of it, and it held in its hand a letter with four seals hanging down from it, on which stood written: I am black, but comely, O ye daughters of Jerusalem, as the tents of Kedar, as the curtains of Solomon: Look not upon me, because I am black, because the sun hath looked upon me, etc But as soon as the *fixum* acted in the *humidum*, a rainbow spanned itself and I thought of the covenant of the Most High, and of the fidelity of my *Ductoris*, and of what I had learned, and lo, with the help of the planet and the fixed stars, the sun overcame the darkness, and over every mountain and valley there came a lovely and bright day; then all fear and terror had an end, and everything beheld this day and rejoiced, praised the Lord, and said: The winter is past, the rain is over and gone; the flowers appear on the earth; the time of the singing of birds is come, and the voice of the turtle is heard in our land; the fig tree putteth forth her green figs, and the vines with the tender grape give a good smell. Therefore let us make haste to take the foxes, the little foxes that spoil the vines, that we may gather the grapes in time and with them make and drink wine, and be fed at the right time with milk and honey-comb: that we may eat and be filled. And after the day was done and the evening fell, the whole heaven grew pale, and the seven stars rose with yellow rays and pursued their natural courses through the night, until in the morning they were overshadowed by the breaking of the sun's red dawn. And behold, the Wise who dwelt in the land arose from their slumber, looked heavenward, and said: Who is she that looketh forth as the morning, fair as the moon, clear as the sun, and there is no spot in her, for her ardor is fiery and not unlike a flame of the Lord: so that no water may extinguish the love, nor any river drown it; therefore we will not leave her, for she is our sister, and though she is yet little, and hath no breasts, we will bring her again into her mother's house, into a shining hall, where she hath been before, to suck her mother's breasts Then she will come forth like a tower of David, built with ramparts whereon hang a thousand shields, and many arms of the mighty men; and as she went forth the daughter praised her openly, and the queens and the concubines spake well of her: but I fell upon my face, thanked God, and praised His Holy Name

---

EPILOGUS

And thus is brought to a close, ye beloved and true *Sapientiae et doctrinae filii*, in all its power and its glory, the great secret of the Wise, and the revelation of the Spirit, about which the Prince and Monarch *Theoph in Apocalypsi Hermetis* saith: It is a single *Numen*, a divine, wondrous, and holy office, while it incloseth the whole world within it, and will become true with all else, and truly overcometh the elements and the five substances. Eye hath not seen, nor hath ear heard, neither have entered the heart of any man, how the heaven hath naturally embodied to truth of this Spirit, in it the truth doth stand alone, therefore it is called: the voice of truth To this power Adam and the other patriarchs, Abraham, Isaac, and Jacob, owed their bodily health, their long life, and finally prospered in great wealth thereby. With the aid of this Spirit, the *Philosophi* founded the seven free arts, and acquired their wealth therewith. With it Noah built the Ark, Moses the Tabernacle, and Solomon the Temple and through this provided the golden vessels from pure gold in the Temple, and for the glory of God, Solomon also wrought with it many fine works and did other great deeds. With it Esdras again established the Commandment; and with it Miriam, the sister of Moses, was hospitable. And this Spirit was much used and very common amongst the prophets of the Old Testament. Likewise it is a medicine and a cure for all things, and the final revelation, the final and highest secret of Nature. It is the Spirit of the Lord which hath filled the sphere of the earthly kingdom, and moved upon the face of the waters in the beginning The world could neither understand nor grasp it without the secret gracious inspiration of the Holy Ghost, or without secret teaching. For the whole world longeth for it because of its great powers, which cannot be appreciated enough by men, and for which the saints have sought from the creation of the world, and have fervently desired to see For this Spirit goeth into the seven planets, raiseth the clouds, and dispelleth the mists, giveth light to all things, transformeth everything into gold and silver, giveth health and abundance, treasures, cleanseth leprosy, cureth dropsy and gout, cleareth the face, prolongeth life, strengtheneth the sorrowful, healeth the sick and all the afflicted, yea, it is a secret of all secrets, one secret thing of all secret things, and healing and medicine for all things.

Likewise it is and remaineth unfathomable in nature, and endless power and an invincible might and glory, that is a passionate craving for knowledge, and a lovely thing of all things which are beneath the circle of the moon, with which Nature is made strong, and the heart with all members is renewed, and kept in blossoming youth, age is driven away, weakness destroyed, and the entire world refreshed

Likewise this Spirit is a spirit chosen above all other heavenly things or spirits, which giveth health, luck, joy, peace, love, expelling altogether all evil, destroying poverty and misery, and also causing that one can neither talk nor think evil; it giveth to men what they desire from the depths of their hearts, worldly honor and long life to the godly, but eternal punishment to the evil-doers, who put it to improper use

To the Most High Almighty God who hath created this art and who hath also been pleased to reveal this knowledge unto me, a miserable, sinful man, through a promise and true vow, to Him be given praise, honor, glory, and thanks, with an entirely humble and fervent prayer that He will direct my heart, mind, and senses through His Holy Ghost, so governing that I talk to no one about this secret, much less communicate it to some one who doth not fear God, nor reveal it to any other creature, lest I break my vow and oath, and break the heavenly seals, and thus become a perjured Brother *Aurae Crucis*, and utterly offend the Divine Majesty, and thereby commit and perpetrate knowingly an unpardonable mighty sin against the Holy Ghost. Wherefore may God the Father, Son, and Holy Ghost, the Most Blessed Trinity, mercifully preserve and protect me constantly. Amen. Amen. Amen.

FINIS.

A Speech of an unknown Philosophi,
dedicated to the fraternity (R. C.)
being
A short discourse or brief example of the holy Philosophiae and most high medicine.

The Most Holy Trinity or Lord God Jehovah

hath made everything out of nothing.
And the Spirit of God moved upon the face of the waters or Chaos:
This being the primum HYLE of the philosophers, or the water out of which everything was created:
Firmament, Mineralia, Vegetabilia, Animalia;

The Great World,

out of its Center and Quintessence.

The Small World,

as the Creator's most perfect creature, namely

The Human-Being,

an image of the Most High God.
The immortal Soul: a heavenly invisible fire.

He has Apostatised: but behold: there is the MESSIAH!

The light of Mercy and of Nature.
LILI; the first matter of the perfect body,
The Mother, giving birth to the middle-world,
Balsam and Mummy.
And the incomparable magical lode stone in the small world.
The philosopher's water from which proceedeth all things, in which are all things, which governs all things in which one errs and in which one is also lead toward betterment
A sane mind in a sane body.
Unceasing prayer,
Patience and waiting
Matter, container, furnace, fire, boiling, is one and only one thing.
Alone in one, and the itself one alone, beginning, middle and end
It does not let any foreign thing come near, is being made without foreign matter.
For see: in the Mercurio is everything for which the philosophers seek

The Small Crystal Clear Fountain.

The twofold Mercurius.
A spin of the sphere and all planets,
And a substance that in an instant is black-smoking from a
GLEAMING

Death and Life.

The rebirth and renewal,
Beginning, middle and end of the fixation or stability,
and the main foundation of the entire magical secret
Take the Quintessence of the Macro and Microcosmi, or Philosophical Mercurii,
The invisible heavenly living fire,
The salt of the metals ana q. s
Make out of it, according to the philosophical art of a Magi, through rotating, dissolving, coagulating and figuring

The Highest Medicine

in which
The greatest wisdom, most perfect health and sufficient wealth.
All from one, and all to one.
Lying and bragging belongs into hell.
Enough is said.
Plain and honest, eliminating all evil, which, is a hindering of the Pathmos.
It shall come to pass, according to JEHOVA'S will.

TO GOD ALONE BE THE GLORY.

Per ignem demum
Nomen & Aetas
PAULUS.

Ω

Lege.

Judica.

A

Tace.

Perceive ye, how strangely the Lord leaveth His Saints. **Psalm 4.**

Since everything left to us in the Holy Scriptures was intended for our study,
Act. 14. v. 17. research and remembrance, so that we humans may fully understand our great
Cap. 17.v.27.28. incomprehensible God and his noble creation, all creatures, and that we might
know ourselves best of all, and since the wondrous ciphers Three, Four and
Ps.104.148.150. Seven are mentioned often in the Holy Bible, these having hidden, undoubtedly,
a great secret.

Therefore I ask in all simplicity and out of a pure heart, what do these numbers convey to us in the light of Nature and in the light of Mercy.

About the Cipher Three.

Firstly, what the three different days signify, Gen. 8, in which Noah let fly out of his ark the raven and after three times seven days the dove.

Secondly, what the very first sacrifice signified, which the Lord God Himself commanded Abraham to give him, about which we read in Gen. 15.

And thus the Lord God spoke unto me

The Divine Theological Mercy-Light,

the spiritual Malach.

Cap. 4.

the Root of Jesse,

Bring me and he brought.
Sun { of 3 years old } an heifer / a she goat / a ram
——n——n

testifies about the Natural Philosophical Light,

the Root of all Metals.

And a turtle dove and a young pigeon, = = Eagles Gluten.
And he took unto him all these and divided them in the midst = Solutio Philosoph.
But the birds divided he not, = = = = = = Sophist. Separatio.
And when the fowls came down upon the carcass Abram drove them away. Caput. Mortum.

Hermetis Bird ☿ eats of the dead carcass also and flies away with it, is finally captured by the Philosopho, strangled and killed.

Thirdly, what signifies the strange holy fire had been, which fell down from heaven, kindling and consuming the sacrifices on the altar. Lev. 9. and 2 Chron. 7. This fire the priests took with them when they were led away into the Babylonian captivity, and they were commanded by the Prophet Nehemiah, also called Jeremiah, to hide the holy fire in a cave, until they again returned home; and then have the priests look for it; but instead of the fire, they found a dense water, but as soon as they poured it over the wood and sacrifice it was ignited by the Sun and the sacrifice and the wood were devoured by the water and the fire. Read 2 Maccab. 1. v. 19. 20. concerning this and where to find and to obtain today the same fire and water, which is the Prima Materia or Spiritus Mundi in which the gold is consumed and arises again to new life after the Putrefaction.

Fourthly, what signify the three great wonder-births in the Old and New Testaments, occurring over and again in the course of nature; announced and proclaimed by the Lord God Himself and subsequently by His angels. Firstly the birth of Isaac. Gen. 15. 18. & 21. Then of Samson, Judges 13. After this of John the Baptist, Luke 1. and lastly the most wondrous birth of our Saviour and redeemer Jesus Christ, the Virgin's Son, surpassing by far the other three, Mathew & Luke 1.

Fifthly, what signify and indicate the three parts of the human being, as 1. Spirit 2. Soul 3. Body, about which the Holy Apostle Paul writes in 1 Thess, 5., in the light of Nature and light of Mercy.

And this is something about the Wondrous Cipher.

ABOUT THE WONDROUS CIPHER FOUR.

Light of Nature.

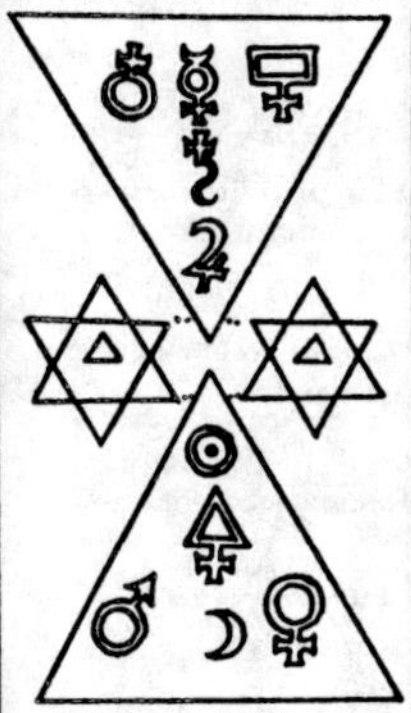

Light of Mercy.

4 Elements.	3 Beginnings.	2 Seeds.	1 Fruit.
4. Fire △ 1.	Sulphur I	Male ☉	Natural becomes 1.
3. Air 2.	Salt 2.	Sperma 2. Sem. 2.	Tincture
2. Water ▽ 3			
1. Earth 4.	Mercury 3.	Female ☽	Supernatural 2.
about God	Nature	Metals	the Art.
God Father	Son	Holy Ghost	Christian

Vae Vae Vae
to you Sophists.

Quinta Essentia.

G. P. W. M.

The fume will rise over you from eternity to eternity and will be your torment.

Who rightly understands this table,
Can see how one originates from the other
First all lie hidden in the fourth cipher
The Elements everywhere,
Out of these originate the three beginnings,
Producing the two sexes,
Male and female, from the Sun and Moon,
The imperial Son grows out of this:
Unequaled in this world,
Surpassing all kingdoms

Firstly, why the Lord God has given three times 40 years respite and time for repentance, to the first world. Gen. 6.

Furthermore, from the Old and the New Testament:

- 40 Days and nights it rained when the flood came upon the earth.
- 40 Days after the flood subsided, Noah opened his Ark.
- 40 Days and nights Moses was upon Mount Sinai.
- 40 Years the children of Israel wandered in the wilderness.
- 40 Days and nights Elijah fasted in the wilderness.
- 40 Days Nineveh had for repentance.
- 40 Weeks it took for Christ and all humans to be formed in their mother's womb.
- 40 Months the Lord preached upon the earth and wrought miracles.
- 40 Days and nights Christ fasted in the wilderness.
- 40 Hours the Lord Christ lay in his tomb.
- 40 Days after His Resurrection He was on earth.
- 40 Years after His Ressurrection and Ascension Jerusalem was destroyed.

Summa 3 times 4 times 40
is the secret interpretation.

Preliminary work.
1. *Mortificatio & Putrefactio*
2. *Solutio*
3. *Animatio*
4. *Purefactio*
5. *Combinatio: est* תיש *seu* ☿ *duplicatus.*

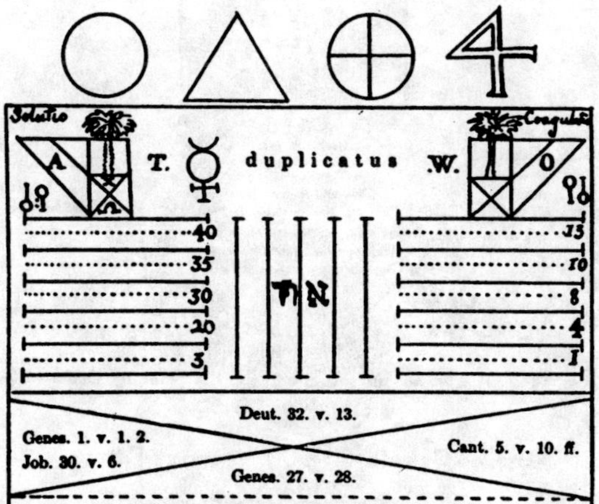

The Philosophical Furnace.

Subsequent work.
Mortificatio & Putrefactio 1.
Solutio 2.
Animatio 3.
Purefactio 4.
Perfectio seu Fixatio 5.

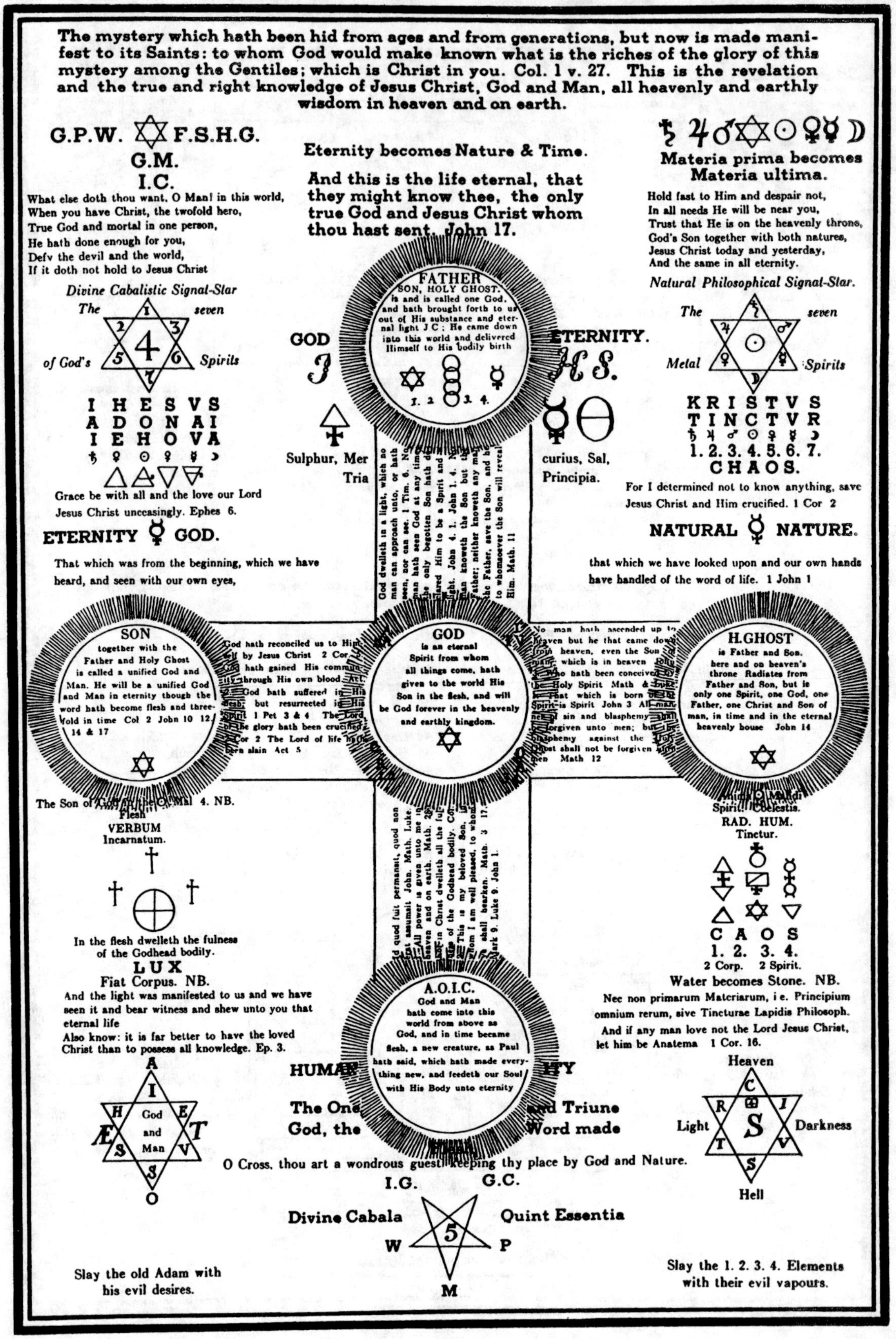
The mystery which hath been hid from ages and from generations, but now is made manifest to its Saints: to whom God would make known what is the riches of the glory of this mystery among the Gentiles; which is Christ in you. Col. 1 v. 27. This is the revelation and the true and right knowledge of Jesus Christ, God and Man, all heavenly and earthly wisdom in heaven and on earth.
G.P.W. F.S.H.G.
G.M.
I.C.
What else doth thou want, O Man! in this world, When you have Christ, the twofold hero, True God and mortal in one person, He hath done enough for you, Defy the devil and the world, If it doth not hold to Jesus Christ
Divine Cabalistic Signal-Star
The seven of God's Spirits
I H E S V S
A D O N A I
I E H O V A
Grace be with all and the love our Lord Jesus Christ unceasingly. Ephes 6.
ETERNITY ☿ GOD.
That which was from the beginning, which we have heard, and seen with our own eyes,
Eternity becomes Nature & Time.
And this is the life eternal, that they might know thee, the only true God and Jesus Christ whom thou hast sent. John 17.
FATHER
SON, HOLY GHOST. is and is called one God, and hath brought forth to us out of His substance and eternal light J C; He came down into this world and delivered Himself to His bodily birth
1. 2. 3. 4.
GOD
ETERNITY.
Sulphur, Mercurius, Sal, Tria Principia.
Materia prima becomes Materia ultima.
Hold fast to Him and despair not, In all needs He will be near you, Trust that He is on the heavenly throne, God's Son together with both natures, Jesus Christ today and yesterday, And the same in all eternity.
Natural Philosophical Signal-Star.
The seven Metal Spirits
K R I S T V S
T I N C T V R
1. 2. 3. 4. 5. 6. 7.
CHAOS.
For I determined not to know anything, save Jesus Christ and Him crucified. 1 Cor 2
NATURAL ☿ NATURE.
that which we have looked upon and our own hands have handled of the word of life. 1 John 1
SON
together with the Father and Holy Ghost is called a unified God and Man. He will be a unified God and Man in eternity though the word hath become flesh and threefold in time Col 2 John 10 12, 14 & 17
God hath reconciled us to Himself by Jesus Christ 2 Cor. 5 God hath gained His community through His own blood. Act. 20 God hath suffered in His flesh, but resurrected in His Spirit 1 Pet 3 & 4 The Lord of the glory hath been crucified 1 Cor 2 The Lord of life hath been slain Act 5
GOD
is an eternal Spirit from whom all things come, hath given to the world His Son in the flesh, and will be God forever in the heavenly and earthly kingdom.
No man hath ascended up to heaven but he that came down from heaven, even the Son of man, which is in heaven John 3. Who hath been conceived by the Holy Spirit Math 1 & Luke 1. That which is born of the Spirit is Spirit John 3 All manner of sin and blasphemy shall be forgiven unto men; but the blasphemy against the Holy Ghost shall not be forgiven unto men Math 12
H.GHOST
is Father and Son, here and on heaven's throne Radiates from Father and Son, but is only one Spirit, one God, one Father, one Christ and Son of man, in time and in the eternal heavenly house John 14
The Son of God in the Mal 4. NB.
Flesh
VERBUM
Incarnatum.
In the flesh dwelleth the fulness of the Godhead bodily.
LUX
Fiat Corpus. NB.
And the light was manifested to us and we have seen it and bear witness and shew unto you that eternal life
Also know: it is far better to have the loved Christ than to possess all knowledge. Ep. 3.
Anima Mundi
Spirit. Coelestis.
RAD. HUM.
Tinctur.
C A O S
1. 2. 3. 4.
2 Corp. 2 Spirit.
Water becomes Stone. NB.
Nec non primarum Materiarum, i e. Principium omnium rerum, sive Tincturae Lapidis Philosoph.
And if any man love not the Lord Jesus Christ, let him be Anatema 1 Cor. 16.
A.O.I.C.
God and Man hath come into this world from above as God, and in time became flesh, a new creature, as Paul hath said, which hath made everything new, and feedeth our Soul with His Body unto eternity
HUMANITY
The One and Triune God, the Word made
God and Man
Heaven
Light
Darkness
Hell
O Cross, thou art a wondrous guest keeping thy place by God and Nature.
I.G. G.C.
Divine Cabala
Quint Essentia
W P M
Slay the old Adam with his evil desires.
Slay the 1. 2. 3. 4. Elements with their evil vapours.

ELOHIM
JEHOVAH
GOD
WORD

Fiat

Natura

Primum Mobile.
Prima Materia.
Quinta Essentia.
Quatuor Elementa.
Lapis Philosophorum.

Fire.

According to all Nature consists

Philosophy of sixteen Elements

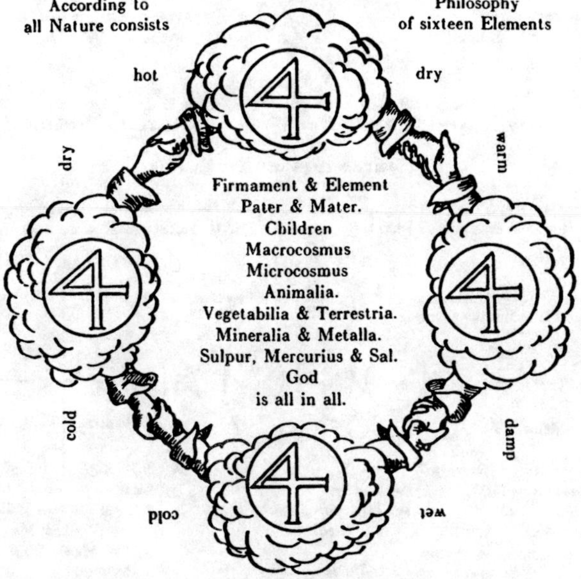

Earth.
Rebis.
Sal.
Chimia.
Corpus.

Air.

CHAOS.
Spiritus Universalis.
Anima Mundi.
Sperma Mundi.
Living Spirit of all Creatures.

Water.
Alchymia.
Azot.
Humidum Radicale.
Hyle.

The Earth was standing out of the Water and in the Water. 2 Pet. 3. 5.

The Spirit of God moved upon the face of the Waters. Gen. I. v. 2.

Ignis Philosophorum
invisibilis & secretissimus occultatum.

Strive for the fire,
Seek the fire:
So thou wilt find the fire,
Light a fire,
Put fire to fire,
Boil fire in fire,
Throw body, soul, spirit into fire:
So shalt thou get dead and living fire,
Out of which will come black, yellow, white and red fire.
Bear thy children in fire,
Feed, give them to drink, nourish them in fire:
So will they live and die in fire,
And be fire and stay in fire.
Their silver and gold will become fire.
Heaven and earth will perish in fire
And become finally a philosophic fire.

Ignis. Q. E. Coelest.

Four times four equals XVI lines,
so many are there of the
ELEMENTS.

Aqua Philosophorum h. e.
Mercurius Primaterialis Catholicus.

Water is water and will be water;
From the heaven of the philosophers water rains;
The philosophers stone cries tear-water,
But the world does not regard such water.
Its fire burns in the water
And lives in the water.
Out of fire make water,
And boil the fire in water:
You will have a fiery water,
Like a sharp salten ocean water.
To children it is a living water,
But consume soul and body to water.
Becomes stinking, green, rotten, blue like heaven water.
Digest, calcinate, dissolve and putrefy the water;
Seek the philosopher's fourfold eternal water
And if done well, the art becomes water.

Aqua Q. E. Secreta.

Four times four equals XVI lines,
so many are there of the
ELEMENTS.

FIGURA CABALISTICA.

The right Reasons for the Wondrous Number of God,

I. 2. 3. 4.

ELOHIM.

O ARCANA ARCANORUM.

The One and Eternal God reveals Himself in the Holy Trinity.

There are three that bear record in Heaven the **F. W. HG.**

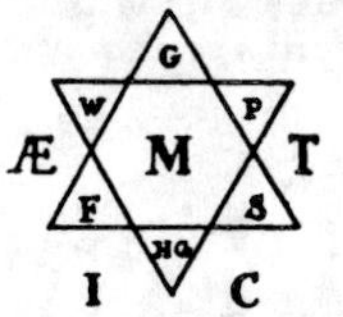

There are three that bear witness in Earth the **S. W. B.**

and these three agree in one. John. 5. v. 7. 8.

After Eternity Heavenly and after Time Creaturally, Naturally.

That is

In Heaven and on Earth

the determined Rosy-Cross apparent to our eyes, and the secret

which the world calls white; of all secrets in Heaven and on Earth.

ETERNAL DIVINE — HEAVENLY — NATURALLY TIMELY

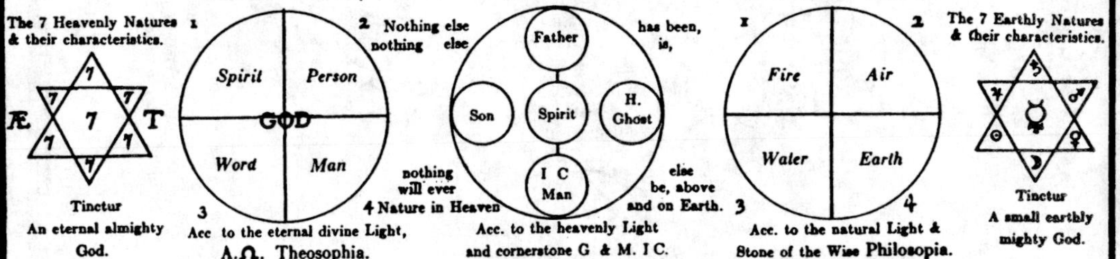

Acc. to the eternal divine Light, A.Ω. Theosophia. Myster. Mag. Acc. to the divine Cabala.

Acc. to the heavenly Light and cornerstone G & M. I C. Theologia.

Acc. to the natural Light & Stone of the Wise Philosopia. Myster. Mag. Acc. to Magia Philosophia.

Explanation of this Holy Figure according to the Alpha and Omega.

	1.	2.	3.		
One God	Spirit,	Person,	Word,	3 Eternal spiritual heavenly Persons -	in one being
	Father.	Son,	Holy Ghost,	3 heavenly timely Persons -	in one being
	God,	Christ,	Man,	3 heavenly and 3 earthly Persons -	in I C. the one human
	1.	2.	3.	who hath suffered and died for all men	1 Tim 2. Act. 3 & 20. 1 Cor 2. Col 2 John 14 1 John 5

The one and three eternal God is a likeness of the entire Nature in all his works and creatures, in

Vegetabilibus — Animalibus — Mineralibus.

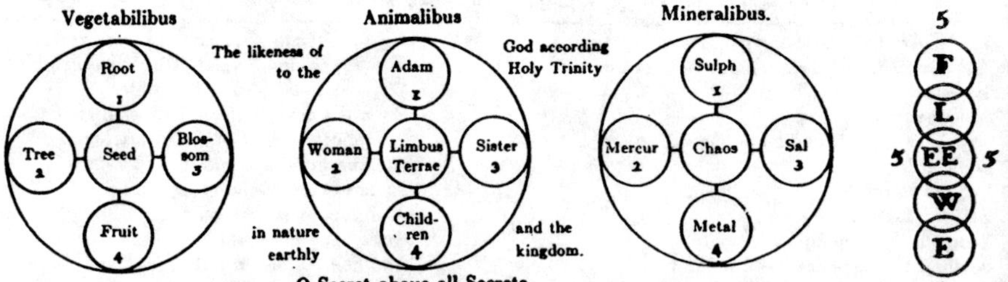

O Secret above all Secrets.

4 *He who truly recognises Jesum Christum hath well employed his time.* 4

The secret wondrous number, i.e., 1. 2. 3. 4., the true Rosy⊕Cross and the revelation and true knowledge of Jesus Christ, God and man, that is all heavenly and earthly wisdom in heaven and on earth. NB. as the one eternal God begot Himself and bore witness of Himself. Three different separate persons and nevertheless is and remains, according to His being, one eternal God, spiritual, heavenly, invisible in eternity as the three heavenly persons: 1. Spirit, 2. Word, 3. Father, one God; and earthly, visible, bodily, a man and God in three persons in time: 1. Spirit, 2. Person, 3. Word, a man; for the Word became flesh, i.e. Eternity became time; God a man; that is, one time, two times and a half a time according to the Old and New testaments, the Law and the Gospel, the heavenly and earthly Trinity, all in heaven and on earth. Since the whole fulness is in Him, J. C., NB. The Godhood itself. Col. 2 and John 9. 10. 12. 14 & 17. Thus speaketh the Heavenly Wisdom: I and the Father are one, believe that the Father is in Me and I in Him, and he that hath seen Me, seeth the Father who hath sent Me and loveth Me, NB. to Him I will manifest myself and the Father and I will come to Him and make mine abode in Him. 1. Cor. 3. & 6. 2 Cor. 6. Eph. 3. 4.

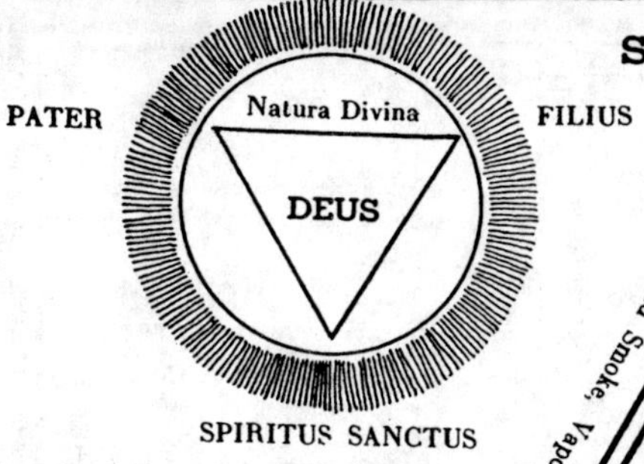

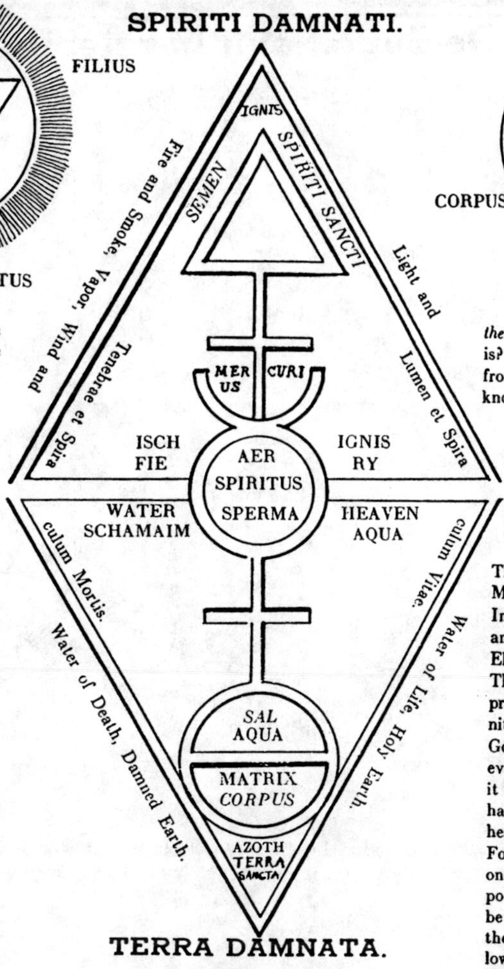

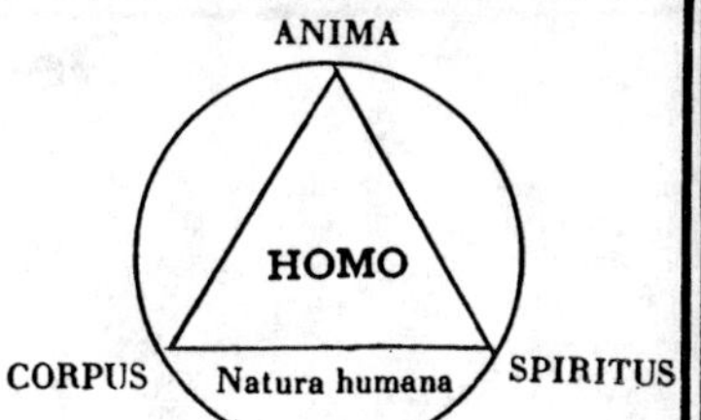

For the Spirit searcheth all things, yea
Who can praise Him as highly as He
many greater ones are still hidden
everything that is and let it be
Syr. 43.

the deep things of God. 1 Cor. 2. v. 10.
is? we see the least of His works, for
from us, for the Lord hath made
known to those who fear Him.

ISAIAH XXVIII.
v.16.

Therefore thus saith the Lord God, Behold, I lay in Zion for a foundation a stone, a tried stone, a precious corner stone, a sure foundation: he that believeth shall not make haste.
Colos. 2. v. 3. In whom are hid all the treasures of wisdom and knowledge.
Ephes. 1. v. 10. That he might gather together in one all things in Christ, both which are in heaven, and which are on earth; even in him.

For thou wilt light my candle: the Lord my God will enlighten my darkness. Psalm XVIII v.28.

So likewise is it in the Parable.

The noble and costly Stone, Misterii Magni and Lapidis Philosophorum. In this Stone lies hidden what God and Eternity, Heaven, Stars and Elements have and are able to do. There hath been none finer nor more precious than this one from all Eternity, and it is offered and given from God to men in his merciful love, and everyone who so desires may get it, it is a stone unsightly to look at, but has in it the power of the entire Godhead.
For compounding and perfecting it one needs 2 central △, in which the power of all things abides; in it must be the very best in heaven and in the world itself, from the upper and lower spheres, which is from far and near, everywhere it can be proved, but not everyone is qualified to do so.

Putrefactio.

Resurrectio.

By steady attendance on the fire and managing it in the right way, one can putrefy, regenerate and perfect the one Universal-Materia in one container and furnace; by one single management of the fires, and Nature does all the work itself, by means of a fire existing within itself, this fire being aroused and revived through the other Philosophic fire. So also the *Laborant* may have nothing else to do besides attending on the fire, pray God for His blessings and benedictions.

With true reason we say that it is Nature itself which rules this art through boiling in its fire and own container. Nature, as far as it is governed by the Heavenly things, till the work be done and even thereafter. But the will is free and may leave Nature to control the result of its work, and set a certain limit beyond which Nature may not go. Since the will rules Nature it should also attract it, but if the will does not attract and is itself subjected to Nature, Nature will go beyond the purposes of the work and destroy the same.

De Septenarii Mysteriis.

This is paradise, bliss, heaven,
born and reborn children of God
eternity. Joh. 17.

eternal life and rest for all new-
here in the time and there in all

ROSEÆ
According to the Theosophia

CRUCIS
and the Theologia.

The secret hidden
world does not know
to say about.

Rosy Cross, which the
and yet has so much

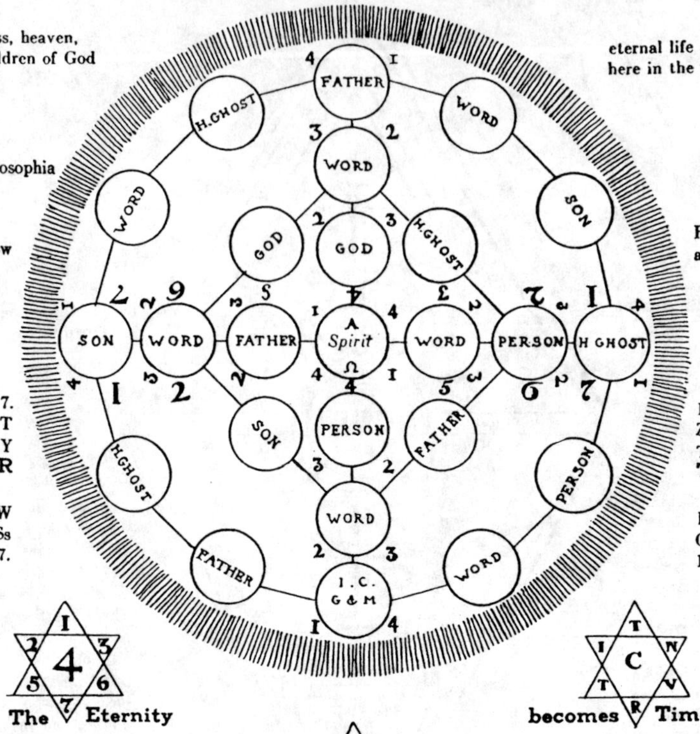

1. 2. 3. 4. 5. 6. 7.
E W I K E I T
E T E R Ni T Y
T I N C T U R
A. O.
O U T F L O W
A U S F L U Ss
1. 2. 3. 4. 5. 6. 7.

1. 2. 3. 4. 5. 6. 7.
Z E I T L I G
T I M E L Y
T I N C T U R
A. O.
I N F L O W
Ge ge n W U R F
1. 2. 3. 4. 5. 6. 7.

The Eternity

becomes Time.

Included in this figure is Eternity and Time, God and Man, Angel and Devil, Heaven and Hell, the Old and the New Jerusalem, together with all creatures, beings, time and hours.

There is a Word speaking eternally,
Self out of itself, in itself, but still not itself,
It may never be spoken out!
Egos, everything, nothing, hell, heaven, earth.
Light, night, good, bad, body, spirit, this, that,
Yes, no, I, thou, give, take, do, let,
Sense, will, reason, no reason, here, there,
Sorrow, joy, scorn, love, quiet, time, eternity,
Soul, angel, devil, life, death, stillness,
Sound, one, none, Man, yes even God.
The Word cannot even reach itself,
Cannot be compared to anything
And yet it is at all times
All in All Jesus Christ!
He speaks, does not speak, is being spoken,
Speaks out, speaks in, remains unspoken,
Creates everything Himself, remains uncreated,
But is Himself what He created:
From the innermost out, from the outermost in,
He has been, is, is not, but will be,
One God, one Lord, one Spirit, one Unit:
Whoever does not believe this,
cannot understand anything,
For from BELIEF comes understanding,
So speaks the Spirit, and writes the Hand,
First believe it, then try it,
If found good, then praise it.
Silentium Sapientiae; Simplicitas Veritatis
SIGILLUM.

12 Patriarchs	12 Stars in the crown Apoc 12
12 Prophets	12 Heavenly signs
12 Apostles.	12 Months in the year
12 Articles of belief.	12 Hours in the day.
12 Gates in the New Jerusalem Apoc 21	12 Hours in the night

PROBAT FIDEM.

The Cross is the best interpretation of the Scriptures.

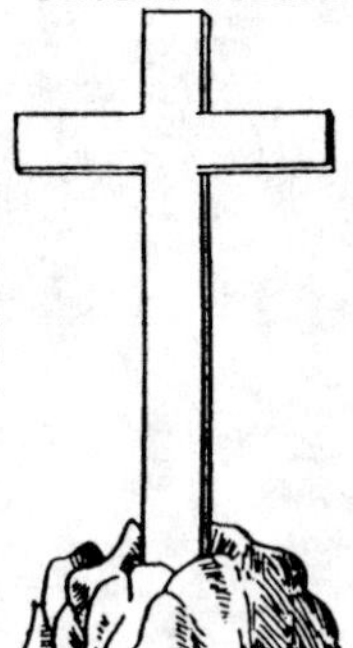

CONSTANTIA.

Animae Pharmaca
Sanctissima Bibliotheca
Lecta placent. Xies repetita placebunt
Via Sancta
SPIRITUS & VITA
Oraculum & Spiraculum
Ie Ho Vae
Rationale Divinarum
AOURIM & TUMMIM
Tabernaculum
DEI cum Hominibus
SANCTUARIUM
יהוה
MEMORIALE
Magnalium DEI
LUCERNA DOMINI
Armarium
Spiritus Sancti
PANACEA
Nectar & Ambrosia
PORTA COELI
LIBER DOMINI
FONS
Signatur
CIBUS ANIMAE
Lumen Gratiae
ORTUS
Conclusus
THESAURUS
Absconditus
VERBUM VITA
Quaerite & Invenietis
Credite & Intelligetis.

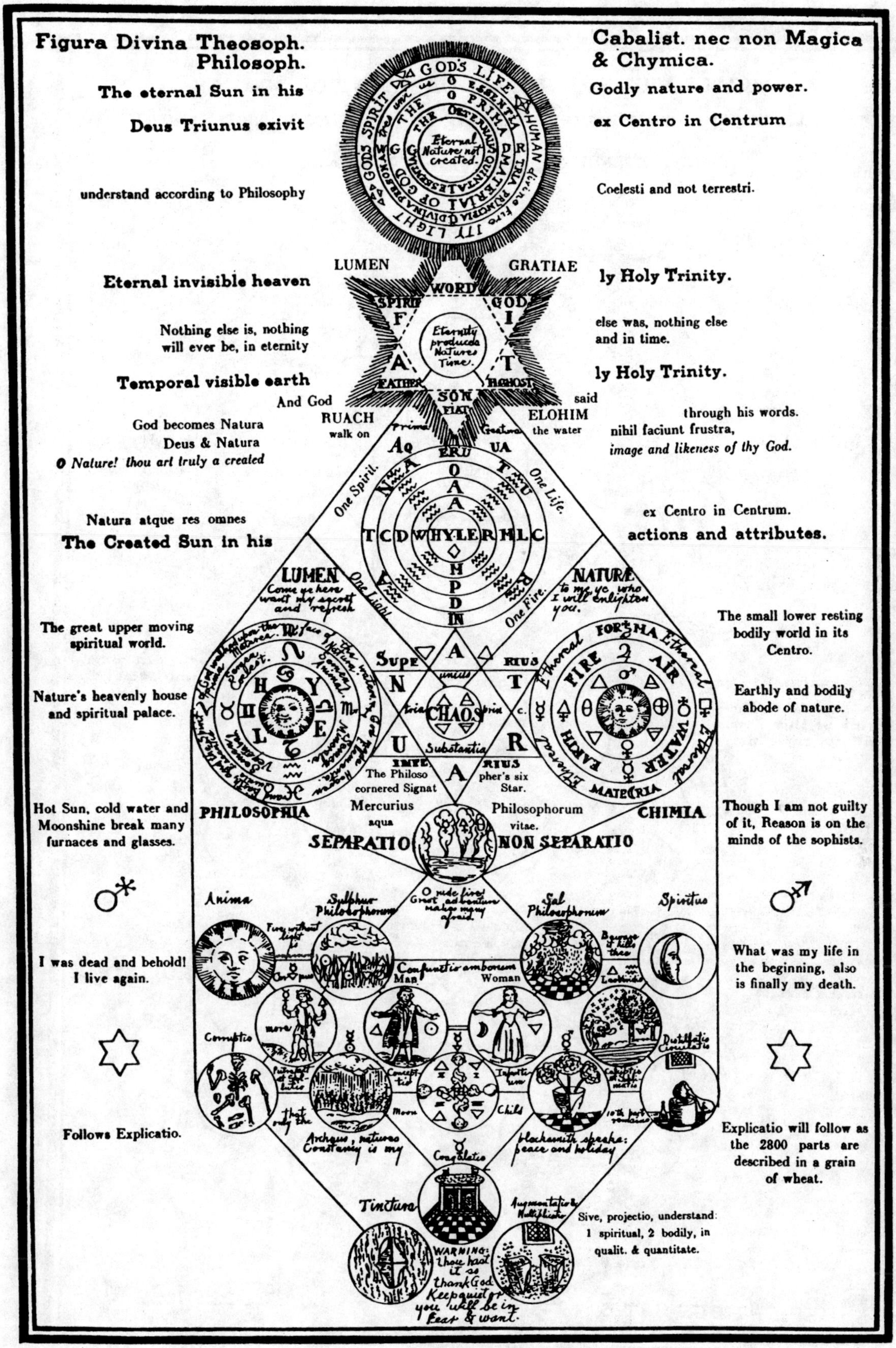
Figura Divina Theosoph. Philosoph.
Cabalist. nec non Magica & Chymica.
The eternal Sun in his
Godly nature and power.
Deus Triunus exivit
ex Centro in Centrum
understand according to Philosophy
Coelesti and not terrestri.
GOD'S LIFE
Eternal Nature not created.
LUMEN
GRATIAE
Eternal invisible heaven
ly Holy Trinity.
WORD
SPIRIT
GOD
FATHER
SON
Eternity produces Natures Time.
Nothing else is, nothing will ever be, in eternity
else was, nothing else and in time.
Temporal visible earth
ly Holy Trinity.
And God
said
RUACH
ELOHIM
walk on
the water
through his words.
God becomes Natura
Deus & Natura
nihil faciunt frustra,
O Nature! thou art truly a created
image and likeness of thy God.
One Spirit.
One Life.
Natura atque res omnes
ex Centro in Centrum.
The Created Sun in his
actions and attributes.
HYLE
LUMEN
NATURE
One Light
One Fire.
The great upper moving spiritual world.
The small lower resting bodily world in its Centro.
Nature's heavenly house and spiritual palace.
Earthly and bodily abode of nature.
CHAOS
Substantia
FIRE
AIR
WATER
EARTH
MATERIA
The Philoso cornered Signat
pher's six Star.
Hot Sun, cold water and Moonshine break many furnaces and glasses.
PHILOSOPHIA
Mercurius aqua
Philosophorum vitae.
CHIMIA
SEPARATIO
NON SEPARATIO
Though I am not guilty of it, Reason is on the minds of the sophists.
Anima
Spiritus
I was dead and behold! I live again.
What was my life in the beginning, also is finally my death.
Man
Woman
Moon
Child
Follows Explicatio.
Explicatio will follow as the 2800 parts are described in a grain of wheat.
Tinctura
Sive, projectio, understand: 1 spiritual, 2 bodily, in qualit. & quantitate.
WARNING: Thou hast it so thank God. Keep quiet or you will be in fear & want.

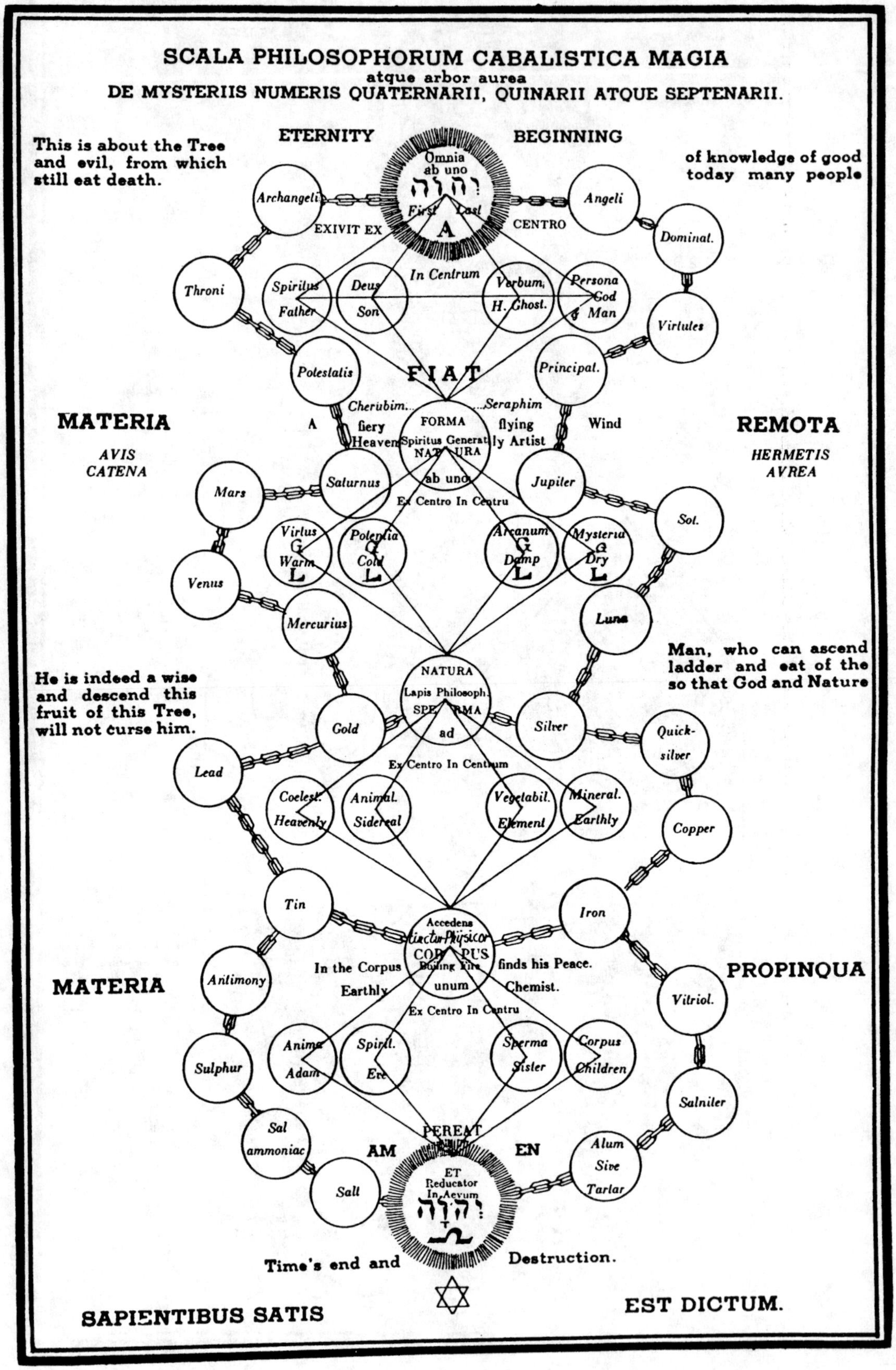

SCALA PHILOSOPHORUM CABALISTICA MAGIA
atque arbor aurea
DE MYSTERIIS NUMERIS QUATERNARII, QUINARII ATQUE SEPTENARII.
ETERNITY
BEGINNING
This is about the Tree of knowledge of good and evil, from which today many people still eat death.
Omnia ab uno
יהוה
First Last
A
EXIVIT EX
CENTRO
Archangeli
Angeli
Dominat.
Throni
Spiritus Father
Deus Son
In Centrum
Verbum, H. Ghost.
Persona God & Man
Virtutes
Potestatis
FIAT
Principat.
Cherubim...
...Seraphim
A
fiery Heaven
FORMA
Spiritus Generat
NATURA
ab uno
flying ly Artist
Wind
MATERIA
AVIS CATENA
REMOTA
HERMETIS AVREA
Saturnus
Jupiter
Mars
Ex Centro In Centru
Sol.
Virtus G Warm L
Potentia G Cold L
Arcanum G Damp L
Mysteria G Dry L
Venus
Mercurius
Luna
Man, who can ascend and descend this ladder and eat of the fruit of this Tree, so that God and Nature will not curse him.
He is indeed a wise
NATURA
Lapis Philosoph.
SPERMA
ad
Gold
Silver
Quick-silver
Lead
Ex Centro In Centrum
Coelest. Heavenly
Animal. Sidereal
Vegetabil. Element
Mineral. Earthly
Copper
Tin
Iron
Accedens
Tinctur Physicor
CORPUS
Burning Fire
unum
In the Corpus Earthly
finds his Peace. Chemist.
MATERIA
PROPINQUA
Antimony
Vitriol.
Ex Centro In Centru
Anima Adam
Spirit. Eve
Sperma Sister
Corpus Children
Sulphur
Salniter
Sal ammoniac
PEREAT
AM
EN
Alum Sive Tartar
Salt
ET Reducator In Aevum
יהוה
Time's end and Destruction.
SAPIENTIBUS SATIS
EST DICTUM.

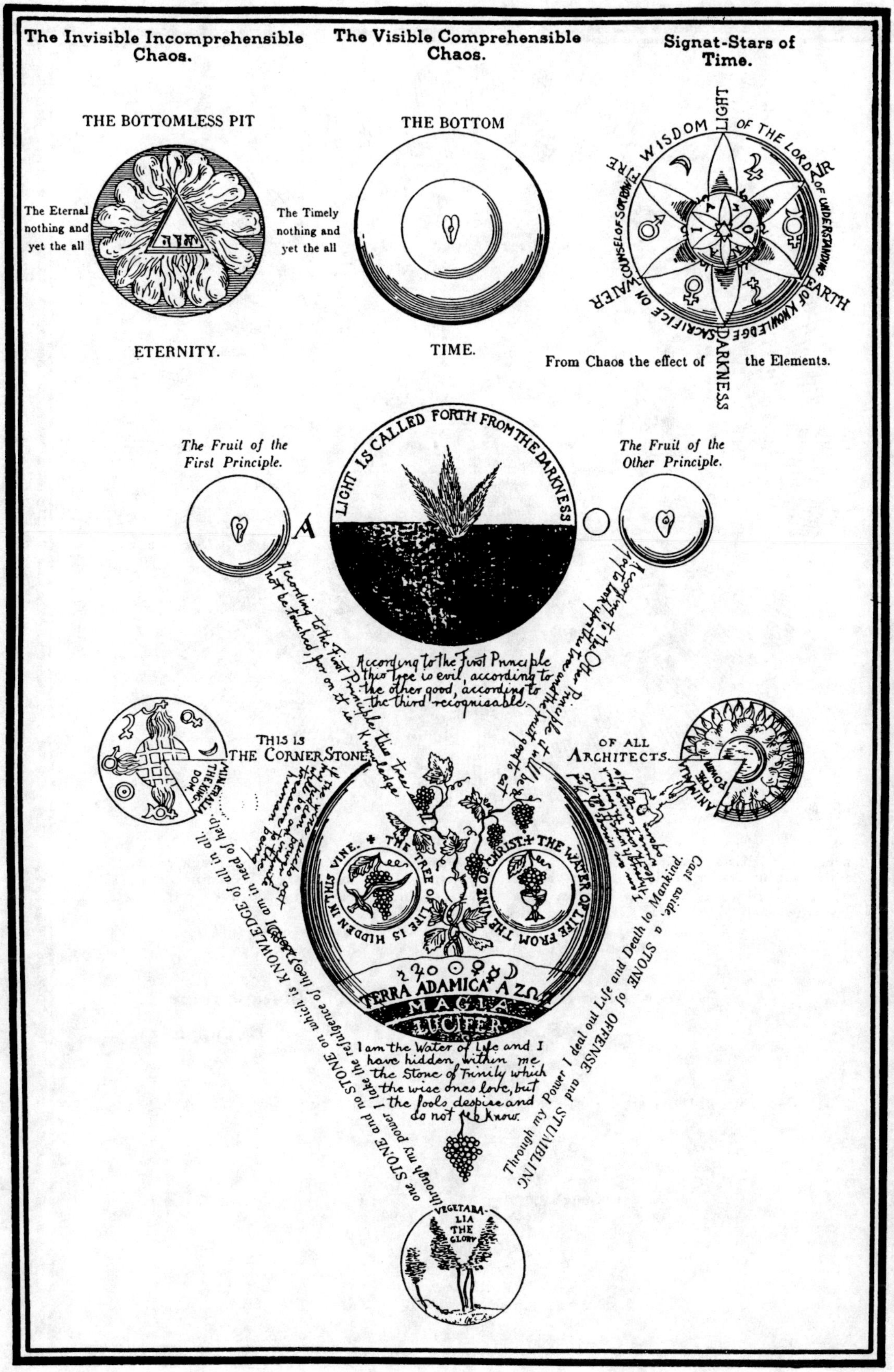

The Invisible Incomprehensible Chaos.
The Visible Comprehensible Chaos.
Signat-Stars of Time.
THE BOTTOMLESS PIT
The Eternal nothing and yet the all
ETERNITY.
THE BOTTOM
The Timely nothing and yet the all
TIME.
WISDOM
LIGHT
OF THE LORD
AIR
OF UNDERSTANDING
EARTH
OF KNOWLEDGE
SACRIFICE ON
WATER
COUNSEL OF SORROW
FIRE
DARKNESS
From Chaos the effect of the Elements.
The Fruit of the First Principle.
LIGHT IS CALLED FORTH FROM THE DARKNESS
The Fruit of the Other Principle.
According to the First Principle this tree is evil, according to the other good, according to the third recognisable.
THIS IS THE CORNER STONE
OF ALL ARCHITECTS
THE TREE OF LIFE IS HIDDEN IN THE VINE.
THE WATER OF LIFE FROM THE VINE OF CHRIST.
TERRA ADAMICA
MAGIA
LUCIFER
I am the Water of Life and I have hidden within me the Stone of Trinity which the wise ones love, but the fools despise and do not know.
Through my Power I deal out Life and Death to Mankind.
Cast aside, a STONE of OFFENSE and STUMBLING
Through my power I take the refulgence of the STONE on which is KNOWLEDGE of all in all.
VEGETABALIA THE GLORY

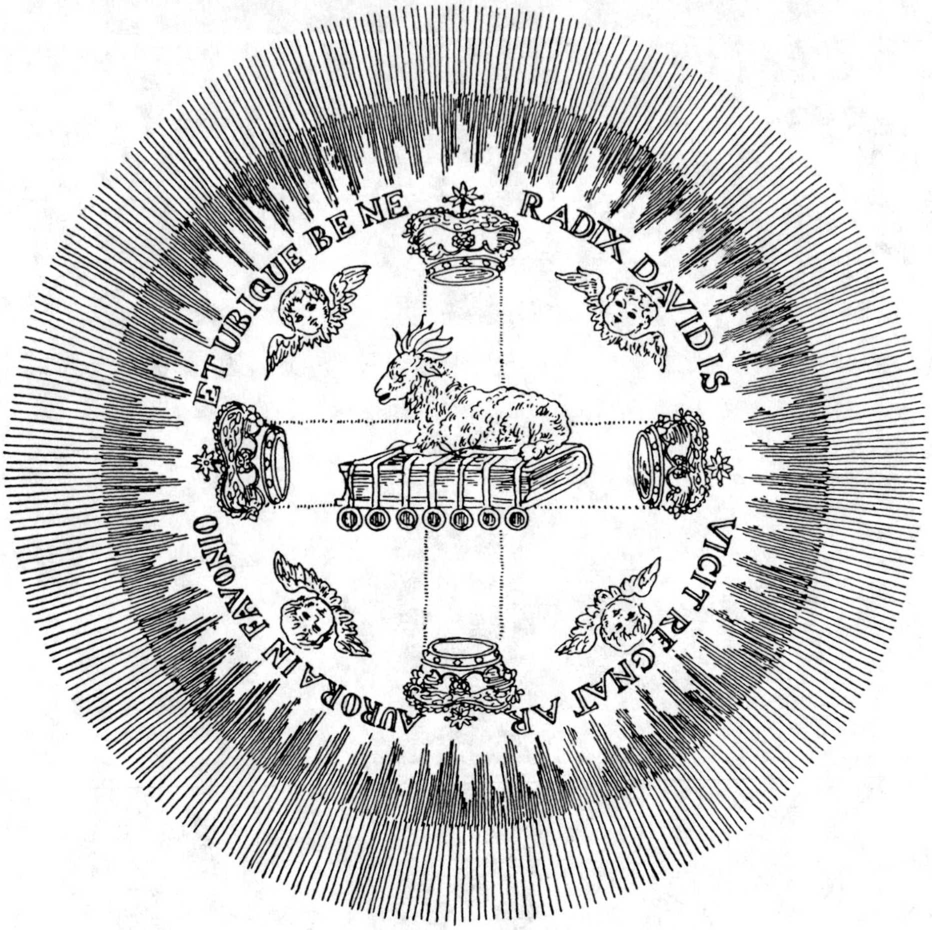

JESUS.

I know nothing, I can do nothing, I do not want anything, I do not please myself, I do not praise myself, I do not relish anything, I do not learn, I do not seek, I do not desire anything in heaven and on earth; only the living word alone, which became flesh, JESUS CHRIST, and him CRUCIFIED. 1 COR. 2.

This is the most holy, most understanding heavenly ARTICUL, and openly revealed to us through God Himself in the Light of Nature.

Physica.	**I am the Alpha and Omega the First and the Last.**	**Metaphysica & Hyperphysica.**

Apocal. 1. v. 11. 12. Cap. 5. v. 5. seq

D. O. M. A.

Deo omnipotenti sit Laus, Honos & Gloria in Seculorum Secula, Amen.

Mea

in Cruce  **Rosea**

Victoria

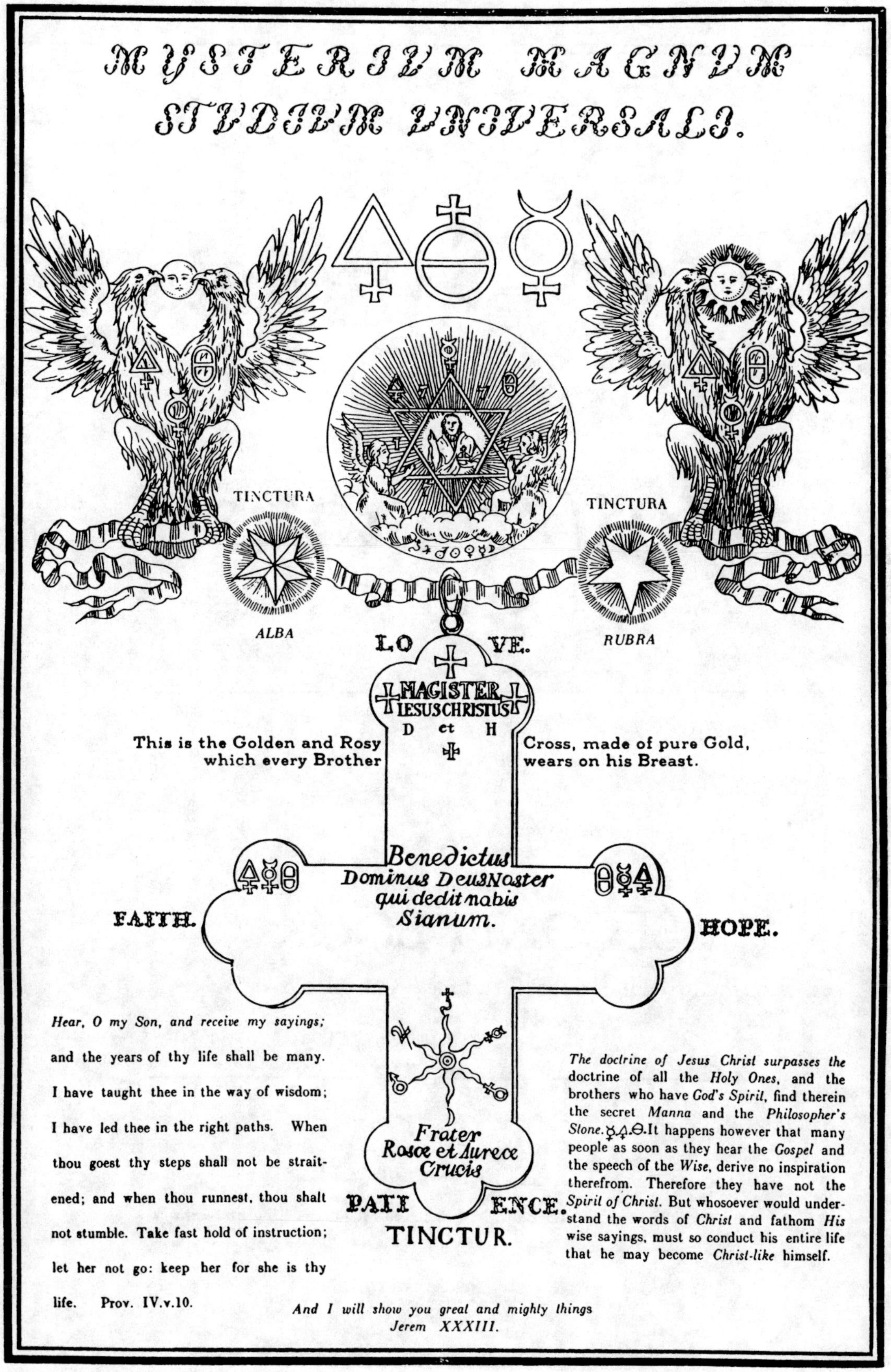
MYSTERIUM MAGNUM
STUDIUM UNIVERSALI.
TINCTURA
TINCTURA
ALBA
RUBRA
LO VE.
MAGISTER
IESUS CHRISTUS
D et H
This is the Golden and Rosy Cross, made of pure Gold, which every Brother wears on his Breast.
Benedictus Dominus Deus Noster qui dedit nobis Signum.
FAITH.
HOPE.
Hear, O my Son, and receive my sayings; and the years of thy life shall be many. I have taught thee in the way of wisdom; I have led thee in the right paths. When thou goest thy steps shall not be straitened; and when thou runnest, thou shalt not stumble. Take fast hold of instruction; let her not go: keep her for she is thy life. Prov. IV.v.10.
Frater Rosae et Aureae Crucis
PATI ENCE.
TINCTUR.
The doctrine of Jesus Christ surpasses the doctrine of all the Holy Ones, and the brothers who have God's Spirit, find therein the secret Manna and the Philosopher's Stone. It happens however that many people as soon as they hear the Gospel and the speech of the Wise, derive no inspiration therefrom. Therefore they have not the Spirit of Christ. But whosoever would understand the words of Christ and fathom His wise sayings, must so conduct his entire life that he may become Christ-like himself.
And I will show you great and mighty things
Jerem XXXIII.

Secret Symbols of the Rosicrucians

of the 16th & 17th Centuries

SECOND BOOK

Brought to light for the first time from an old manuscript

ALTONA, 1788

Printed and edited by J. D. A. Eckhardt, Prin ter to H. M. the King of Denmark

A Golden Treatise About the Philosopher's Stone

BY A STILL LIVING BUT UNKNOWN *PHILOSOPHER*. FOR THE INSTRUCTION OF THE *FILII DOCTRINAE*, AND FOR THE INFORMATION OF THE *FRATRES AUREAE CRUCIS*

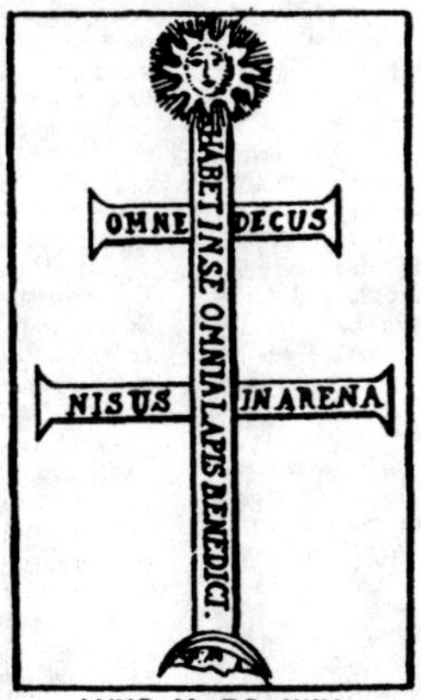

ANNO M DC. XXV.

FOREWORD

To The Reader In Search Of The Art

Be not surprised, my dear Reader and honest Investigator of Nature's Secrets, that I should undertake to write this short Treatise when in this final age the world standeth with one foot already in the grave, while close at hand many libraries are found full of books which are written about this *Materia*, the majority of which, however, instill a false philosophy and give fictitious formulae. I have not written for my own sake, but for thy sake, to show thee the ground of truth, and to lead thee from wrong ways which seem important to thee. As far as I am concerned, I already know what is necessary for me to know of this, hence I have no need of books. For in the past twenty-two years I have read as many as I could lay hands on, and there have been not a few written as well as printed. Thou wilt find described herein the *Materia* and the *Solution theorice*, and also the entire *praxis* in its *allegoria* wilt thou find completely implied, as plainly and clearly as thou mayest hope to find from any Philosopher. I have studiously applied myself to consult thereon with the *Philosophi*, and I have called attention to all the places where they have mentioned this or that aphorism, so that thou mayest thyself see, look up their books, compare both the *concept* and my *allegata*, and sharpen thine understanding with it. Now I might have written this Treatise with much less effort by omitting my *allegata*, and could have made myself known to the *Fratres aureae crucis*; but, as said before, it is all for the best that thou mayest gather more understanding therefrom. Thou shouldest not be surprised that I have kept my name hidden and that I do not reveal myself to thee personally; for I do not seek vain honor, and I am not intent on making a great name for myself in this world, but I am thinking only of thy profit. Besides, my Masters, the true *Philosophi*, taught me not to risk my life at all for the sake of fame, and offer myself to greedy robbers, and load great sins upon myself by prostituting this great secret. They who taught me this were the true *Philosophi*, my Teachers The reader will learn from *Sendivogius* that as often as he doth reveal himself to the great lords it is every time to his hurt and to the increase of danger. And experience proves that different *Philosophi* who did not take sufficient care of their treasures, were choked to death and robbed of their *Tincture* by greedy and vain fellows who risked their souls for that purpose. Reason asserteth that whoever carrieth so great a treasure with him doth not like to be robbed of it. *Sendivogius* concealed his name in his *Anagramatismis*. A short time ago a new *Frater aureae crucis* also made himself known in an *Anagramata* and *Aenigmata*, and his name is well known to me. Why then should I lay myself bare before the whole world? Let this be sufficient for thee, dear friend, that I make myself known to the Wise, and at the same time withhold my name from thee, which I have then done without fault, commending the rest to our Lord God, who will reveal me to thee if it should please Him, and if it should be advantageous to me and to thee Do not let thyself long to search out my name; for even if thou shouldest ever find it and should know me, thou wouldest still have to be content with this *Treatise*. For I have sworn with *Bernhardus of Trevisan* and other *Philosophi*, in all justice to reveal nothing more than is done here. And do not be concerned at all about whether I have this treasure in my hands But rather ask if I have seen how the world was created? How the darkness came over Egypt? What is the cause of the rainbow? How the transfigured bodies will look after the Day of Judgment? Which is the most constant color? But I ask of you who understand my booklet whether ye have seen the great and universal salty sea, without any corrosive matter, which is in itself sufficient to carry the *Tinctures* of all things up onto the highest mountains? Tell me, Where doth Sulphur become Sulphur, and where doth Mercury come forth from Mercury? Likewise, where will Sulphur come forth from Mercury, and Mercury from Sulphur? When have your eyes beheld the symbol of ardent love, as when man and woman so embrace each other that they will be no more separated through all eternity, but become one in glorious love? Do ye understand now what I am talking about? If ye have worked out these things with your own hands, and beheld with your own eyes, then am I your consociate, and make known to you that I also know, and that I like nothing better than to receive your secret message; for that purpose I want to write this little Treatise.

But if anyone should complain about the difficulty of this art, then let him know that this art in itself is not difficult at all, that it will be easy for those who love God and who are by Him deemed worthy of it, will find it quite easy.

However, if some one should accuse me of having written all too plainly and clearly about the art, so that everyone could understand it: to him I answer that it is true that I have written about it lucidly enough for those who were found worthy in God's sight, but the unworthy will do well to leave it alone I have previously set forth the entire art, word for word, to the over-clever ones, but they ridiculed it in their hearts, and did not believe that in our work was a twofold resurrection from the dead Therefore is our art in *Theoria* and *practica*, a pure gift of God, who giveth it to whom, and when, He will, and it doth not depend on any man's willing or doing. I have known it with all *circumstantiae*, and manipulations for fully seventeen or eighteen years, and yet I had to wait until it pleased God to bestow upon me His grace Also, no one should doubt the certainty and truth of this art, especially since it is as true, as certain in Nature and as undoubtedly ordered by God as that the sun shineth by day and the moon by night Herewith I shall bring to a close this little *Praefatio*, and begin with the *Treatise* itself. But you, my beloved *Fratri aureae crucis*, who have now and then kept yourselves hidden in secret and enjoy the gifts of the High God in His fear, hearken unto my words, and hide not from me, and if so be you know me not, let it be known to you that the Cross trieth out the faithful and revealeth their faith in the light of day, but such are kept hidden for the sake of safety and delight. God be with us all AMEN.

Dear beloved Reader and Follower of the True Wisdom: The old and new *Philosophi*, after they attained the goal of their desires through divine grace, took care in their writings to make themselves known to their fellow-students, who kept themselves hidden here and there in the world, and to indicate to them how the true God had enlightened their understanding, blessed the work of their hands, and revealed to them the great secret of earthly wisdom Wherefore they rightly pledged themselves to give Him all praise, honor, and glory And then also they promised that they would bequeath to their fellow-Christians and art-seeking disciples at the same time instruction and information, so that they might at once thereby might also love and be loved by God, and attain to understanding and knowledge of such *Secreta*.

And there have been such people amongst all nations, such as the Egyptians, the most eminent of whom was *Hermes Trismegistus*, the Chaldeans, Greeks, Arabs, Italians, French, English, Spaniards, Germans, Poles, Hungarians, Jews, and many others. There is nothing surprising about it, although the said Wise Men wrote in different languages at different times, there is nevertheless unity and agreement and general *consensus* to be found in their writings, that every true Philosopher could soon recognise that God had favored them with His great blessing, and that they had had the Work itself in their own hands And just as truth manifesteth itself in *Harmonia*, so on the contrary must *Dissonantia* bring every Sophist and supposed Philosophers into the open

For while he never rightly knoweth the secret of the Wise and pursueth his way according to his own mind, every man who is cognisant of the art will see his error

But *Harmonia* and concord especially consist mainly of these two points, *viz.*, in knowledge of the *Materia*, their *Solution*, weight, fire, and *Augmentation* With respect to the *Materia*, it is such that it hath within itself everything which is necessary for it, hence all that the lover of the art desireth will be made of it, namely *nisus in arena*, as the *Philosopher Anastratus* saith in the *Turba Philosophorum*: There is nothing more precious than the red sand of the sea, and this is the Monn's saliva, which is added to the Sun's light and *Coagulated*.

But that such a unified *Materia* is necessary, *Agadmon* himself testified, saying: Know that if ye do not take my *Corpus*, which hath no spirit, ye will not obtain what ye are looking for: and this because no alien substances shall come into your work, and know also that nothing else is required for it except that which is pure. Therefore renounce all multiplicity. For Nature is satisfied with only one thing, and whosoever doth not know that, he will perish. Even likewise doth *Arnoldus de Villanove* express himself in his booklet called *Flos florum*: Our stone is made out of one thing and is made with one thing. Likewise doth he say to the King of *Neopolis*: Everything contained in our stone is essential to its existence, and it doth not have need of anything else, especially since the stone is of one nature and one thing. And *Rosinus* saith: Be thou sure that it is only one thing, whereof everything is made that thou dost desire. And *Lilius*: Thou art in need of but the one thing, which changeth into a different nature at every step of our work. Also saith *Geber* in his *Summa*: It is but one stone, one medicine, to which we add nothing, and from which we take nothing, only separating the superfluous from it. And *Scites* saith in the *Turba*: *The foundation* of this art is something that is stronger and higher than any other thing, and is called the sharp vinegar, which is the cause of the gold becoming a pure spirit, without which neither whiteness, blackness, nor redness could exist: and when it is mixed with the body, then it becometh one with the body, and transformeth it into a spirit, and it coloreth it with spiritual and unchangeable color, and receiveth from that which is colored its bodily color in turn, which cannot be obliterated: and if thou shouldst out the body into the fire without the vinegar, then it would be consumed.

But some one might draw the conclusion from the sayings of *Scites* that not one but two things are required, namely: the body and the vinegar, as he calleth it; and it is necessary that a moist and a dry be joined together, so that the dry will not be consumed by the fire, but will be protected by the moisture from the burning fire. I must truly consent to such *Argument* and conclusion, if it be rightly understood, but nevertheless I must maintain the above-mentioned philosophical sayings in their merit and truth. Because it is certain for one thing that the one *Materia* of our blessed stone hath many names amongst the Philosophers, which Nature hath prepared for the artist, and for the *Materia* of the great stone alone, and hath ordained otherwise nothing else in the world.

This is before the eyes of everyone, the entire world seeth it, apprehendeth it, loveth it, but still doth not comprehend it. It is noble and bad, dear and cheap, costly and low-priced, and is found everywhere. *Theophrastus Paracelsus* calleth it the "Red Lion" in his book *De Tinctura Physica*, much mentioned, but little known. *Hermes*, in his book, chapter 1, calleth it: Mercury, which is hardened in the innermost cells. In the *Turba* it is sometimes named *Aes* or Ore: in the *Rosario Philosophorum it* is called Salt. In the *Summa* this *Materia* hath as many names as there are things in this world. That is the reason why it is so little understood by the ignorant. I call them ignorant because they proceed to the art without previous knowledge of Nature and her qualities: as *Arnoldus* saith: They proceed like an ass going to its manger, and which doth not know what it is going to receive into its opened mouth.

Therefore in his *Summa perfectionis*, *Geber* saith truly and rightly: He who hath no knowledge by himself of the beginning of Nature is still far from this art. And *Rosarius* saith: I advise that no one commit himself to finding this art save he who hath knowledge of the beginning of true Nature and its order: then when he hath knowledge of this he doth not need more than this one thing, and it doth not require great expense. For it is not more than a stone, a medicine, a phial, an order, and a preparation. Thus will our *Materia* be separated with the help of Nature and the intelligent manipulations of the *Artisan*, so that it will be transmuted into the "White Eagle," as *Theophrastus* saith, and the radiance of the *Sol* doth not shine after the *Spagyrization*, or (as *Basilius Valentinus* saith) out of it cometh a spirit as white as snow and another spirit as red as blood, both of which spirits have the third hidden within themselves. King *Aros* spake well when he said: Our medicine will be one substance made out of two, namely out of the unification of the constant, of the spiritual and bodily, of the cold and moist, warm and dry nature, and it cannot be made out of anything else. And *Richardus Anglicus* saith: It is a stone and a medicine made out of the *Philosophis* Rebis, *i. e.*, out of two things, namely, out of the body and the spirit, white or red; and many fools have erred therein by explaining in many different ways the verse: *Est rebis in dictis rectissima norma figuris*. That is, two things, and these two things are one thing, namely: the water added to the body, and such dissolved in a spirit, that is, into a mineral water out of the body and spirit, which is the Elixir that is called a *Fermentum*. For then the water and the spirit are one thing from which is made the *Tincture* and medicine in which all bodies are purified. Therefore our medicine is compounded out of one thing, this being the water and the spirit of the body. And so we have, according to the *Philosophi*, the nature of Sulphur and Mercury above the earth, from which are made gold and silver beneath the earth. And *Bernhardus, Count of Trevisan*, saith: Our work is taken raw from one root and two mercurial substances and is drawn, clean and pure, from the *Minera*, etc. And in his book *Concerning Natural and Supernatural Things*, *Basilius Valentinus* saith in the 4th chapter: I will reveal unto thee truthfully and through the love of God, that there is to be found the root of the philosophical Sulphur, which is a heavenly spirit, together with the root of the spiritual but natural *Mercurii*, which is the beginning of the spiritual salt in one, and is found in one *Materia*, out of which the Stone, destined for me, was made, and not in many things. And although Mercury by itself is found by all Philosophers, and Sulphur by itself, and Salt is drawn particularly from itself, so *Mercurius* will be found in one element, Sulphur in one, and Salt in one. Nevertheless I say unto thee that they arise only out of their superfluity, which is found most plentifully and can be used *particulariter* in many ways with advantage, and be prepared for medicine and for transmutation of metals. But the *Universal* alone is the highest earthly treasure, and all three things in their beginning are one thing only, and will at the same time be found in one thing only and extracted therefrom, which can make one out of all metals; and this is the true *Spiritus Mercurii* and *Anima Sulphuris* including the Spiritual Salt at the same time united and enclosed under one heaven and dwelling in one body, and this is the Dragon and the Eagle, it is the King and the Lion, it is the Spirit and the Corpse, which must color the corpse of the Gold into a Medicine, etc. So now our prepared *Materia* is called the man and the woman.

Likewise with respect to the working and the suffering, *Zimon* saith in the *Turba*: Know ye that the secret of this work existeth in the man and the woman, *i.e.*, in the producing and suffering. In lead is the man, in *Auripigment* is the woman. The man rejoiceth over the woman whom he hath received unto himself, and she helpeth him, and the woman receiveth from the man a coloring seed and is colored by him. And *Diamedes* saith: Join together the manly son of the Red Knight to his fragrant wife, and thus joined together they will beget the Art, to which there should be added no alien matter nor powder nor any other thing, and be ye content with the conception: so shall the true son be born unto you. Oh, how precious is the *Materia* of the Red Knight, without whom no order can exist! Others call it *Argentum vivum* or *Mercurius* and *Sulphur* or Fire. As *Rogerius Baco* saith in *Speculum Alchemiae*, chapter 3: All metals are born out of *Sulphur* and *Mercurius*, and nothing is connected with them, for if nothing be added to them, nothing will change them save what is derived from them. Therefore we must rightly take *Mercurius* and *Sulphur* for the *Materia* of the stone. And *Menabadus* saith: Whosoever addeth Mercury to the body of *Magnesia* and the Male to the Female, draweth out the hidden nature, with which the bodies will be colored.

And *Lullius* saith in his *Codicil*: It is the quality of our *Mercurius* that it letteth itself be coagulated by its Sulphur. And in the *Practica* of his *Testament* he saith: The Mercury is an overflowing and running moisture, thus preserved from the burning. Others call it body, spirit, soul. Thus *Arnoldus* in *Flos florum* saith: The *Philosophi* have said that our stone is composed at the same time from body, soul, and spirit, and they have spoken the truth. For they have compared the unperfected *Corpus* to the body, because it is weak. They have called the water spirit, and this with truth, as it is a spirit. But to the *Fermentum* they have given the name of soul because it giveth to the unperfected body the life which it did not have before, and it thus produceth a better form. And a little before this he saith: The spirit will not be joined to its body except through the medium of the souls. For the soul is the medium between the body and the spirit, which joineth both together. And *Morienus* saith: The soul quickly entereth its body; but if thou wouldst join it to another body, thou wouldst work in vain. And *Lullius* saith: Soul, spirit, and body are together, and are one thing, which hath everything in itself, to which nothing alien is added. But why is it necessary that one bring up all the names which people call our *Materia* and of explaining them? Let it be sufficient for our purpose to have mentioned the ones most commonly used. And after we have explored where this, our *Materia*, came from and where it will arrive, then we will consider a little the *Solution* as the principal part of the whole art, and through reflection we shall sharpen our reason and understanding.

Proceeding now to the consideration of what our *Materia* is and where it must be obtained: it is to be known that the Almighty Creator, whose wisdom is as great as is He Himself, hath created two things in the beginning, when there was nothing but Himself: the heavenly things and those that are under the heaven. The heavenly things are themselves in heaven, and the heavenly inhabitants, about whom we do not want to have philosophical discourses at this time. The created works under the heavens are produced from four elements, and their numbers are to be found only in three species, namely: first those that have life and feeling, called *Animalia;* then secondly everything which groweth out of the earth but hath not feeling, and called *Vegetabilia*. Finally everything growing beneath the earth, and called *Mineralia*.

Now these three species of creatures comprise everything created out of the four elements under the moon, and neither more nor fewer of them will be found, and the Most High God hath approved of each of them in its species and kind, so that not one of them can be transformed from one kind or species to another. As if one could make a man or a tree out of a stone, or a monkey out of an herb or lead; or out of lead make some other animal or herb. Such, I say, is impossible by decree of the Great King. If such were permitted in Nature, there would be fewer of their kind, yea, one could be transformed into any of the others. But as all would therefore fall into great confusion, the Lord of all lords hath decreed that such a metamorphosis of species shall not be permitted. And what is more, not only hath He preserved the three species, each true to its kind, but He hath hath given to every creature a seed, to increase and reproduce its own likeness with it, and these forms should not be transformed into any other form, as a man into a horse, or an apple tree into lettuce, or a diamond or other stone into gold. So I say: In Nature such things are not permitted. And as it hath been since the beginning, so will it be until the day cometh when the Almighty, as He said in the beginning: Let there be, will say: Let it perish. But it is fully permitted that among the things which have a common *Materia*, seed, and *composition* of the elements, a refinement of their conditions may be accomplished and achieved, according to the purity and perfection of their *Materia*.

Thus one seeth a man who hath a much nobler and intelligent mind, because of the pure and subtle spirits which originate in the justified and well-tempered *Constitution* of the bodies, rising higher than others, who do not have such acute and subtle understanding. So, too, one seeth how one horse is much nobler than another, and the same thing is to be observed in nearly all the *species animalium*. And as is the case with animal species, so is it also found amongst the superabounding herbs and trees. In trees through implanting, grafting, and others means well known to the gardener; amongst the herbs and flowers one can observe every day how one is more noble, more beautiful, more fragrant, better, finer tasting than the other; one hath only to look upon the *Caryophylli*, or carnations, and the *Tulips*, and I will not say here how many kinds there are, for no one can begin to count them, which, through constant attention and improvement, can be taller and finer, so that some flowers are to be produced so beautiful and fragrant that one might think there had been none of their kind before.

Now what shall I say about the metals? Their common *Materia* is Mercury, which is boiled and coagulated from Sulphur. As *Richardus Anglicus*, chapter 6, saith: The qualities of all liquid and fusible things were wrought by Nature from the essence of Mercury and its Sulphur; for it is the quality of Mercury that it cannot be burned and coagulated by any fumes or heat of red or white Sulphur. And *Arnoldus*, in the first volume, chapter 2, of his *Perfectum Magisterium et Gaudium*, saith: Mercury is the source of all things which can be dissolved, for as soon as a metal is dissolved it turneth into Mercury and can be mixed with it, since it is of the same essence. There is one difference in the *composition* of the said *Corpora* from Mercury, and that is their degree of purity or impurity, the impurity coming from the impure Sulphur, and which is alien and contrary to it. And *Rosinus* saith to *Saratanta*: The *Materia* of all metals is the boiled and imperfect Mercury, which boiled the Sulphur in the belly of the earth, and after the Sulphur hath been separated there are many metals produced in the earth, all of which have in common a single and universal original *Materia*, the only difference between them being that some are more and some are less affected than the others.

Therefore we see daily with our own eyes how Nature taketh pains in assiduous labor to purify all metals and to bring them to greater perfection, which is to make gold of them, that being Nature's final *intention*. So we then see in all metals what Nature beginneth to produce in them: since there are no metals which do not contain a grain of silver or gold. And what is more, it is so done with the metals that Nature forthwith will and can make gold out of Mercury when it hath its Sulphur in itself, when nothing alien cometh between, and the unclean, stinking, and combustible Sulphur doth not prevent it, as we then see, in many places will be found fine and pure gold without being mixed with other metals.

Because in the tunnels there commonly cometh to the Mercury an alien Sulphur, which contaminateth the former and hindereth it in its perfection, so also will be produced different metals after the manner of such alien Sulphurs. For as *Aristotle, 4 Meteorologica*, saith: If the substance of the Mercury is good and the combustible Sulphur impure, so will it turn such into copper. But when the Mercury is calculous, impure, and earthy, and the Sulphur is also impure, then iron will result. It appeareth as if tin had good Mercury, which is pure, but it hath bad and evil Sulphur. But lead hath crude, bad, heavy, glutinous Mercury and a bad, impalatable, and stinking Sulphur, and therefore it is not easy to let it coagulate.

This hindering, combustible, and stinking Sulphur is not the right fire, which doth boil the metals well, but the Mercury hath its own Sulphur, which doth such, and as *Bernhardus Count of Trevisan* saith: Many believe erroneously that in the production of metals a sulphur-like *materia* would be added; but it is evident that in the Mercury, when Nature worketh, is inclosed its own Sulphur: But which doth not prevail in the same, except through warm motion, through which the said Sulphur, and at the same time the other two qualities of the *Mercurii*, are altered. And in this manner are produced in the other different metals of the earth. For in this earth, as *Arnoldus* saith in the first chapter of his *Rosarii*, is a twofold superfluity: One is included in the innermost part of the Mercury, which hath in the beginning mixed itself in its essence: The other, however, is added apart from its nature, and corrupteth it The one can be separated from it with great difficulty; the other, however, will be taken away by no skill of any artist.

Therefore the great heat of the fire separateth the combustible moisture from the metals, because the Mercury holdeth that and preserveth it from combustion, which is its nature, but expelleth the foreign substance from itself and letteth it be destroyed by fire. But the innermost Sulphur, which boileth the Mercury and bringeth it to its perfection, is pure and impure in the same degree, combustible and non-combustible. The combustible keepeth the Mercury from its perfection, so that it should not become gold, until this Sulphur is finally entirely separated therefrom, and constant sulphur alone remaineth therein. Then the mercury will become gold or silver, according as its sulphur is red or white. But this innermost sulphur is nothing else than a timely *Mercurius* or the ripest and most timely part of the Mercury, therefore Mercury readily receiveth it, but leaveth other and alien sulphur behind. For as *Richardus*, chapter 9, saith: The better and purer the sulphur is, the more it relisheth the good and pure Mercury and attacheth itself to it. So that one is more and more closely associated with the other, until more and more perfect metals are produced by this union.

But such sulphur is not to be found above the earth, as saith *Avicenna*, except in those two bodies, namely of gold and silver, and much more mature in the gold *Richardus*, chapter 12, saith: The red sulphur is in the gold through greater maturing, but the white is in the silver through lesser maturing.

Now if all this be so, namely: that there is a single universal *Materia* in all metals, which through its power with innate sulphur, either soon or otherwise, according as it separateth itself through length of time in more steady boiling from the alien and ineffective sulphur of the other metals, becometh gold, which is the goal of the metals, and the perfect purpose of Nature Then we must indeed admit and say that Nature also seeketh and desireth to have, in this species as in the animal and vegetable kingdoms, its improvement and perfection through purification and subtle refinement of the *subjecti* in its own nature.

This now, beloved seeker of the things in Nature, would I explain somewhat more in detail, that thou mayest grasp it much more thoroughly and that thou mayest understand the *Materiam* of our great stone. For if thou wouldest undertake to make for thyself such a stone as ours out of some animal substance, thou wouldst be thwarted, for they both belong to two different species, since the stone is mineral, but the *Materia* is animal. And as *Richardus*, chapter 1, saith: One cannot bring out of anything something that is not in it Therefore, because every species seeketh in its own species its power of increase, and every *genus* or kind seeketh it in its own kind, and every nature seeketh it in its own natural nature, and beareth fruit according to its natural characteristic, and no contrary nature: therefore every collectivity agreeth with its own seed And *Basilius Valentinus* saith: Beware, my friend, and understand that thou shouldest not seek to make use of any animal soul Like thine, their flesh and blood, as it hath been granted and given by the Creator to the animals, belongeth to the animals, therefore God hath at the same time ordained that an animal shall be made out of it.

Therefore they are to be greatly wondered at who, holding themselves to be great artists, look for their *Materiam Lapidis* in *Menstruis muliebribus*, in *Spermate*, in eggs, hair, urine, and in many other things, and fill many books with such recipes, and also convince, deceive, and mislead other foolish folk with such worthless things

And greatly astonished at the folly of such people is *Rogerius Baccho*, in *Speculi*, chapter 3, since he saith: One should greatly marvel that a thoughtful man should base his *intention* upon animal and vegetable things, which are so very widely separated, when one findeth *Minaralia* which are much closer

It is by no means to be credited that any *Philosophus* should have placed the art in such above-mentioned widely separated things, except it be knowingly for the sake of allegory. As *Basilius Valentinus* saith: Our stone doth not come forth from things that are combustible For our stone and its *Materia* are safe from all danger of fire Therefore thou mayest well abstain from searching in animal things, since Nature hath not permitted it to be found in such But if anyone would look for our stone in vegetable things, as in trees, herbs, or flowers, he will err for the above-mentioned reasons, no less than he who would make a great rock out of an animal For all herbs and trees, together with all that cometh out of them, is combustible, and nothing remaineth of them except a mere salt with its earth, which it hath received from Nature in the composition And let no one be mislead because some pretend to be able to make the Philosopher's Stone out of wine or parts thereof. For while they do not understand rightly the writings of *Raymundus Lullius*, they only prove with all their great knowledge that they do not understand anything, and mislead both themselves and others. Of course it is also true that out of these things very splendid and excellent *Menstrua* could be prepared, without which in neither medicine nor in alchemy could anything be undertaken or accomplished But that the Philosopher's Stone could be made therefrom, or its seed be extracted, was not granted to Nature by the Creator, but which, as mentioned above, is ordered to remain true to its kind

Therefore, everyone who hath understanding, can easily deduct and conclude that our stone, which, as said, is incombustible, must be sought and found in an incombustible *Materia*, which is found nowhere except in the mineral kingdom, since animal and vegetable things are all combustible

Because our previously mentioned Philosopher's Stone is a mineral product, one can reasonably ask out of how many kinds of minerals may the stone ultimately be made; for there are as many species as stones, among them divers kinds of substances and earths will have been understood, salts, semi-minerals, and metals.

To this I answer there is reason to believe that it is impossible to make the stone out of any of these, for the reason that there is in all of them no liquid or fusible Mercury, and that they cannot be melted or dissolved into their first *Materiam* on account of the Sulphur in them, which is much too crude and has too great an abundance of Judaic qualities. No intelligent seeker of the natural secrets will seek the *Materiam* of the Philosopher's Stone in salts, alums, and materials of their sort. For he will find in them nothing else than a sharp corroding and destroying spirit, but not the kind of *Mercurium* or *Sulphur* that the *Philosophi* want and need.

But from such things can no intermediate mineral, such as *Magnesia*, *Marcasite*, *Antimonium*, etc., be made. Much less will a metal come from them. How then could one obtain from them the *Materiam* of the Philosopher's Stone, which is the end and perfection of all metals and mineral things? Besides, these have absolutely nothing in common nor any affinity with any metals — nay, rather, they burn, break, and corrupt them; how then could they serve to perfect them? Hear now what *Richardus*

Anglicus, chapter 10, saith hereon: The lesser *Mineralia* cannot change into any metals, in the first place because they are not born of the first *Materia* of all metals, which is *Mercurius*.

But since their origin differs so greatly from the origin of *Mercurii*, in form and *materia* and at the same time in setting, no metals can come forth from them, since there has to be a first substance and seed of a like thing, from which such will be produced. But what is said appeareth clearly therefrom, that the lesser *Mineralia* are not produced from *Mercurio*, as is clear, also, according to *Aristotle* and *Avicenna*. Therefore if they should be transformed into *Metalla*, they would first have to be brought into their first *Materiam*.

But since this cannot be done through any art whatsoever, so there can never be any metals and no final *Materia* of its stone. Wherefore, since the lesser *Mineralia* cannot be in the beginning through the art, which is *Mercurius*, they cannot be in the middle and the end of it, which are the metals and the *Tincture*. But the lesser *Mineralia* are alien to the metals in their nature, and although to some extent they have a part in the mineral power, they are the lesser quality thereof and are combustible. Therefore the metallic nature hath no pleasure in them, but repelleth them and keepeth only what is of its own nature. Wherefore they are fools who bring forth so many and such different deceits, to deceive the people, and they do preposterous things, who neither have Nature with them, nor can they make themselves understood.

And let no one be deceived by the writings of the Philosophers if at times they speak about salts, as when in *Allegoriis Sapientum* it was said: Whosoever laboreth without salts cannot resuscitate dead bodies. And in the book *Soliloquii* it is written: Whoever worketh without salts shooteth with a bow without a string. But they have quite another meaning than mineral salts. As is to be seen clearly in the *Rosario Philosophorum*, where it is said: The salt of the metals is the Philosopher's Stone. For our stone is a coagulated water, in gold or silver, and resisteth the fire, and can be dissolved only in its own water. Geber, in his book about the furnace, chapter 19, teaches that the coagulated water of the philosophers is not mineral water, but their *Mercurius*, saying: Apply thyself to dissolving the dry water of the sun and the moon, which the common man calleth *Mercurium*. The *Philosophi* in their parlance call it salt at times, as is to be seen in *Clangore Buccinae*, where it is said: Note that the *Corpora* is alum and salts, which floweth out of our bodies. Also at times they call the medicine itself salt, as is written in the *Scala*: It is the work of the other water, that it augments the earth in its wondrous salts, through its attracting power alone. And *Arnoldus* saith in his book about the preservation of youth: But that which hath not its equal in preserving youth is the salt out of the *Minera*. The Wise compared it, when it was prepared, to the natural warmth of a healthy youth, and also because of this they have called the stone by the name of an animal; others have called it a mineral *Chifir*, and some have called it an everlasting medicine and *Aquam Vitae*. The entire science of its preparation is that it should be reduced to a pure and drinkable water, with those things which have much the same qualities as it doth.

Hence it is now easy to see that, according to the teaching of the philosophers and also the property of Nature itself, the *Materia* of the stone cannot be taken from the lesser minerals.

Now let us look around a little and see whether the *Materiam* of our great stone can be made out of the semi-minerals, such as *Marcasite*, *Antimony*, *Magnesia*, and others, especially since the *Philosophi* mention this on several occasions. As when *Senior* saith: If there were not in our *Auripigment* the quality of coagulating the *Mercurium*, our mastery would never reach the goal. And *Thomas Aquinas*: Take our *Antimonium* or the captured black earth, etc., and *Parmenides* in the *Turba*: Take Mercury and coagulate it in the body of the *Magnesiae*, or in Sulphur, which is not combustible.

But here, nevertheless, it is to be understood that the *Philosophi* did not so speak to indicate that our great stone could be made out of such things, but they spoke in this manner only by way of allegory. For the philosophical *Auripigment* and *Magnesia* are quite another thing from those of the common people, namely, the *Materia* itself, which they call *Agens*, the Lion, the King, the Sulphur, and many more names; and, what is more, it will be called *Auripigment* because it hath the power of gold in superfluous color, and it is called *Magnesia* because of its great virtue and glory, which emanateth from it.

But when *Thomas Aquinas* calleth it *Antinomium*, he doth so because of its black and glittering color, which it taketh on after its dissolving. For when our stone became black, it was compared to all black things by the *Philosophi*

Here some one might talk to us and say: That of these semi-minerals some were produced not only from *Mercury* and *Sulphur*, but also became metals: as one sees Magnesia or Bismuth succeed in being mixed with lead or tin.

Likewise, not only doth the *Antimonium* mix with metals, but it becometh a natural lead So also have people of low and high degree occasionally seen it become gold Could one not obtain from it the *Materia* of the stone, since it was produced from *Mercury* and *Sulphur*, into which it can be reduced again through art, and is of one origin with all metals? To this I answer: First, one hast to distinguish between the semi-minerals, namely, between those which have by themselves a *Mercurium* and those which have it not. One hast to pay close attention to those which have *Mercury*, because, through our medicine, their *Mercury* can be changed into gold and silver, and therefore, as I claim, they have to be regarded as half metals, *i.e.*, as minerals disposed to turn to metals. The others which have no *Mercury* are not to be considered at all. But on account of the bad and combustible Sulphur which is found in them, and which is the reason that the *Antinomium* is opposed to all metals and burneth them all except the gold, which because of its constancy it hath to leave in peace, so here one cannot come so far, one cannot select them for the *Materiam* of our stone, which must be pure and delicate and incombustible Sulphur. But on close examination and testing, one can easily see that they are impure and thoroughly infected with their Sulphur.

Zinc appeareth, from its brightness, weight, outer looks, and feeling like pure *Mercurium*, but as soon as it cometh into fire it dissolveth into smoke, vanishing like a pale yellow Sulphur. The *Marcasites* cannot be forced to melt at all because of their great earthy impurity. The *Antimonium*, however, can be cleared of its over-great blackness through skilled manipulations and be brought into a white and beautiful *Regulum*, and it appeareth to all as if something great could be made out of it, therefore many people, who otherwise deem themselves to be very clever, believe that the Philosopher's Stone can be made out of it. But however much one may clear the *Antinomium* from its blackness, there still remaineth in it crude and inflexible Sulphur which appeareth when it doth not let itself be expanded under the hammer and become malleable, which is the quality of every metal, by which, together with other qualities, it is known to be a metal.

In addition to that, it hath a crude and impure *Mercurium*; I do not wish to say now that it retaineth within itself at any time a dissolving Sulphur. And I hope that they do not mind that I cannot agree with their point of view who call themselves great *Philosophi* and want to convince themselves and others in many books and widely circulated writings, that at just this point is the *Scrupel* of their *Universal*. For one seeketh foolishly for something in a thing where it is not. As *Arnoldus* saith: Because it is established in the practice of the *Turba* that the Philosopher's Stone is of a pure *Materia*. So also saith *Lullius* in his last Testament: Our *Tincture* is only a pure fire. And in the *Vade Mecum* he saith: It is the subtle Spirit alone which tingeth and thus cleareth the *Corpora* from their leprosy; but the *Minerals*, however, which are crude and impure like the other can in no way be cleansed in their innermost except by means of our *Tincture*: and therefore one can not obtain from them the *Materiam* of our stone. For *Richardus*, chapter 1, saith: Nothing can be taken, out of a thing which is not therein.

What shall one say about the *Vitriol?* Through its wonderful qualities it bringeth many into error, especially since a part of it can be changed into copper, and it can also change iron into copper. Let it be known that *Vitriol* is nothing else than a beginning and *Materia* of copper. In the veins of the earth fire-damp and vaporous *Mercurius* are found in a place where in great quantity hath been found a bitter and astringent venereal *Sulphur* which, as soon as it was mixed therewith, hath coagulated and tried to become a metal. But because Nature wanted to separate the pure from the impure, the combustible from the incombustible, the abundance and manifoldness of the abovementioned Sulphur have exceeded the *quantitas* thus far. So also in such separation the *Mercurius* had to separate itself and had to let itself be concealed in the vitriolic green.

This can be seen clearly: that one addeth a common Sulphur to the copper is the cause of its destruction and calcineth it; for art accomplisheth with strong fires in a short time what Nature must perform with slow-burning fire. Then the copper will be entirely consumed, and bringeth this into the vitriolic order through general manipulations: and according as there is much or little Sulphur, the *Vitriol* will be richer or poorer in colors. Therefore that is the reason that some *Vitriol* hath more copper qualities than the other: one findeth much copper in the cyprian Vitriol, less in others.

It is to be well noted that the sour *Spiritus* in the *Vitriol* cometh from the Sulphur, especially since it can be found likewise and extracted from common Sulphur. The sulphur-like smell can be well observed in the *Spiritu Vitrioli*, and the *Spiritus Sulphuris* can change the *Sulphur Martis* into a Vitriol, like the *Spiritus Vitrioli*. But because in iron there is also a crude Sulphur, the corrosiveness of the Vitriol eateth such away, seeketh its *Mercurium* which is not much unlike its own, and through union of it with its Sulphur, becometh a good, malleable copper.

But because there is in Vitriol such a crude, superfluous Sulphur, and because there is but very little Mercury in it, and which has not yet arrived at its purification, we shall not get more out of it than out of the other. And we have to heed the teaching of *Alphidius* who saith: My son, beware, separate thyself from the dead bodies and stones; therein is no way to walk, since their life is not being augmented but diminished, as are the Salts, *Auripigmenta*, arsenic, magnesia, marcasite, and the like.

And *Arnoldus*, in *Flore florum*, saith: The cause of their error is that the four spirits, namely, *Auripigment*, *Salmiac*, *Mercurius*, and *Sulphur*, are not the seed of either the perfect or the imperfect metals, with the exception of *Mercury* and *Sulphur*, which coagulateth the *Mercurium*.

Now some one might conclude from these last words of *Arnoldus*, that common Sulphur and Mercury are the *Materia* of our stone, because such are counted among the four spirits, and because the Sulphur coagulateth the Mercury. Hereupon I must ask with *Richardo*, chapter 11: Whether every Sulphur will coagulate Mercury? To this I answer: No! For every common Sulphur, as the *Philosophi* say, is opposed to the metals. It is to be known that Sulphur was produced from the fat of the earth in the depths of the earth, and hath been made solid by moderate boiling, and then it is called Sulphur.

There are two kinds of Sulphur: living and combustible. The living Sulphur is the effectual part of the metals and when cleansed by Nature of all impurities, the *Materia* of our stone, but of this more later. But the common or combustible Sulphur of metals or *lapidis Materia*, but their enemy. For, say *Avicenna* and *Richardus Anglicus*, the common and combustible Sulphur doth not belong to our masterly skill, because it did not originate from it. For white as art can make it, it infecteth at all times, maketh black, and corrupteth everything made of it, for it is a destroying fire.

Therefore it preventeth fluidity, when it is fixed. The example of this we see in iron, which hath in itself a constant, crude, and impure Sulphur But if it be burned, it becometh an earthy substance, like a dead powder. Now how could this give life to others? For it hath a twofold superfluity, namely, one that can be set on fire, and the earthy one

Now consider the common Sulphur, not the Sulphur of the Philosophers which is a simple, live fire, which reviveth other dead bodies, and bringeth them to maturity. Therefore common Sulphur cannot be the *Materia* of our stone. But what shall we say about common Mercury? Of which all *Philosophi* say that the *Materia* of our stone is a mercurial substance and hath very many qualities which will be attributed to our Mercury. For it is the source of everything which letteth itself be fused, as *Arnoldus, Ros. lib.* 1, *cap.* 2, saith: Every fusible thing, when it is melted, will be transformed into it, and it mixeth itself with them because it is their substance; albeit the bodies differ at the same time in their composition from Mercury, according to their purity or impurity, and would have retained alien Sulphur And in chapter 4 he saith: The *Mercurius vivus* is clear in all its effects, that most perfect and constant thing, for it withstandeth burning and causeth liquifaction, when it hath been fixed, and is the *Tincture* of a red superfluous perfection, of glittering appearance, and doth not cease from the mixture so long as it lasteth; and it is friendly and sociable and the means of joining together the *Tinctures* since it letteth itself be thoroughly mixed, and adhereth to their innermost, hence it is of their nature. There is one, and one only, which the fire conquereth, but it will not be conquered by the fire, yet rejoiceth in it and remaineth in it.

And *Bernhardus* saith: Most precisely do we follow Nature, which hath in its lodes no other *Materiam* wherein it operateth other than the pure mercurial form In this *Mercurius* now is hidden the constant and non-combustible Sulphur, which bringeth our work to perfection, without any other substance save for the pure mercurial substance Since there are such splendid qualities in the *Mercurius*, must it not certainly follow that the *Materia* of our stone must be in this? To this we answer: That as there are two kinds of Sulphur, there are also two kinds of Mercury: the common and the philosophical The common *Mercurius* is still a crude, untimely and open *Corpus*, which cannot remain in fire like the philosophical, since through a moderate heat it is turned into smoke and will quickly vanish Therefore the *Philosophi* also say in common parlance: Our Mercury is not a common mercury. So *Lullius* also saith in his *Clavicula*, chapter 1. We say that the common mercury cannot be the mercury of the Philosophers, whatsoever may be the art with which it is prepared: for one cannot keep the common in fire, therefore it is done through another bodily mercury, which is warm, dry, and more timely

But most of the Philosophers have written according to their superfluity about the sublimation and other preparation of the common mercury: wherefore many queer books about this subject have come into existence, so that people learned more and more about the nature and character of this subject, but the purpose they had aimed at, namely, the great treasure of earthly wisdom, no one hath as yet ever been able to find in their writings, because Nature hath not placed it therein But in truth, it is so peculiar in its work that it would mislead one who calleth himself a Wise Man. For example, I knew one who had amalgamated it with gold and handled it so subtly that he brought it through all the colors unto *Citrination*

In this color it stood, and he, thinking he had it fixed, put some more fire under it, thinking he could not go wrong in putting fire under it after the manner of the *Philosophi* Whereupon the glass burst, and the *Mercurius* went up the chimney, taking with it all the gold, gilding the chimney with it And he had to scrape the gold out of the chimney and reduce it again.

It hath also been seen that the common *Mercurius* as a *Corpus* itself can neither open another *Corpus*, namely the gold, nor work therein, even if many colors let themselves be perceived in it, whilst the heat worketh its effect in moisture. But had this good man realised, as many others have done, what *Arnoldus* saith in *Flore florum*, such would not have happened to him. For *Arnoldus*, when he discourses about such alchemists, saith: When they considered this more subtly, they found that mercury is the origin and source of all metals, and with sulphuric and boiling heat, they sublimated the *Mercurius* for themselves, then they fashioned it, they excluded it, and coagulated it, but when they came to the projection, they found nothing, etc.

Therefore we cannot consider common mercury as the *Materia* for our stone Thus far we have sough for the *Materia* for our stone in animals, vegetables, and in stone, in the lesser minerals, and also in the semi- and greater minerals, but we have not found it so far, and we must therefore look further, whether we can find it in metals, and if it should be therein, whether it is in all of them at once, or only in some of them, and if so, in which they are to be found This has long been known, and *Rogerius Baco* doth assert in his *Speculo*, chapter 3, all metals are produced out of Sulphur and Mercury. And one cannot take away or add anything to them, and cannot change them, except what cometh from them, since every improvement augmenteth the nature of the thing from which it cometh. As *Richardus*, chapter 1, saith: As it also is otherwise in all Nature, everything is ordained by the Highest Creator, so that each thing doth bring forth and bear its own kind. And as dumb animals cannot bring forth their kind to any increase except through the nature of their own kind, so is it with everything else in Nature. Therefore *Basilius Valentinus* saith: Thou art not permitted to look for the true stone, nor shalt thou undertake to make it, except out of its own seed, out of which our stone hath been made even from the beginning.

To find this seed, thou must consider by thyself for what purpose thou dost want to find the stone, and then it will become obvious to thee that it can come only from a metallic root, from which the Creator commanded all metals to bear and come forth. There is a great similarity between the production of metals and that of the great stone, especially since there is Sulphur and Mercury in both, as well as the Salt, and the noble soul hath concealed itself, and one cannot possibly obtain the advantage of use in metallic form until these three are brought together in one, after having been taken out of metallic substance, and after this nothing must be added which doth not come from them And therefore it is plain, as *Baccho* saith, that no thing which hath not had its origin in Mercury and Sulphur can be sufficient to perfect them and transform them Therefore it is necessary for the production of the great stone that a metallic substance be taken But whether one can find this in the imperfect metals remaineth to be seen.

There are many to be found who want to find the white in lead or tin, and the red in copper or iron, or the *Materia Lapidis* in both; without doubt mislead by the *Philosophi* themselves For thus saith *Geber in Lib. Fornac.*, chapter 9: As customary, the dough that is to be fermented we extract out of imperfect bodies And therefore we give thee a general rule: that the white dough is to be extracted from *Jupiter* and *Saturn*, but the red from *Venus*, *Saturn*, and *Mars*. So also doth *Basilius Valentinus*, in his book about natural and supernatural things, teach that a *Tincture* can be made out of the *Conjunction of Mars and Venus*

Likewise in his *Triumphal Chariot*, he saith: After this followeth the *Tinctura Solis et Lunae*, etc., from white, then the *Tinctura Vitrioli* or *Veneris*, and likewise the *Tinctura Martis*, both of which have in them the *Tinctura Solis*, if they have been brought before to permanent fixation. Then followeth the *Tinctura Jovis and Saturni* unto the Coagulation of *Mercury*, and then the *Tinctura Mecurii* itself.

Now let this be known to the investigators of natural secrets, that such hath not been the opinion of *Geber* and *Basilius Valentinus* or other Philosophers, else they would contradict themselves, which cannot be, since the Wise must always tell the truth in their writings, although they may mask the truth in concealing phrases For there can come forth perfection neither in the imperfect metals nor amongst those which are so mixed with each other that they could at least be improved Out of those things themselves alone such cannot come, because for our stone the purest essence of Mercury is required, as *Clangor Buccinae*, *Avicenna*, *Lullius*, and in general all Philosophers say: We must choose for our Work the purest Mercurial substance But the purest substance of Mercury is not to be found in the imperfect metals of Nature, because they are like leprous bodies, which are corrupted and rendered inactive by alien and impure Sulphur, so that no kind of art can bring them to their inner and perfect purification, and they cannot even stand fire And it is a necessary quality of our *Materia* that it remain constant in fire, which does not occur here

Let us now hear what *Geber* hath to say in his *Summa*, chapter 63, about this impurity of the imperfect metals and the qualities of the perfect Mercury: Herein we found by true experimentation a peculiar kind of two secrets, *viz.*, one secret is that there are three causes for the destruction through fire of every imperfect metal, the first of which is that their combustible Sulphur is inclosed in their innermost part, and is enkindled with a strong fire, lesseneth the entire substance of the bodies, transformeth them into smoke, and finally consumeth them, however excellent their Mercury may be

The second cause is that the outer flame is augmented by them, passeth through them, and dissolveth them into smoke, however dense they may be

The third cause is that their bodies may be opened through the Calcination, for then the flame of the fire can pass through them and transform them into smoke, however perfect they may be. Now when all these causes of destruction come together, then necessarily the bodies will be destroyed and reduced to nothing But when they are not together then the speed of the destruction of the bodies is less rapid. The second kind of these secrets concerneth the quality of the Mercury in these bodies. For since in Mercury there is no cause of destruction or expulsion, it doth not separate the compound into parts, but remaineth with its entire substance in the fire. For this reason one hath necessarily to recognise the reason of its perfection. Let us therefore praise and give glory unto God the All-Highest, who hath created the Mercury and given it its substance, and to the substance those qualities which cannot be found in the other things of Nature, that therein the perfection may be brought about by some art, and which we find therein in its nearest power (*potentia proquinqua*). For this it is that overcometh fire and is not overcome by it, but remaineth friendly therein and rejoiceth in it.

In these words Geber proveth infallibly that the *Materia* of our stone cannot be in the imperfect metals, because they are themselves impure, and if one wanted to purify them they would completely disappear therefrom. But our *Mercurius*, on account of its purity, is constant in fire and cannot be damaged by it.

Now since these imperfect metals cannot be the *Materia* of our stone, much less can they be such when mixed together, for they become not purer than they were before through their mixture. And in addition to this cometh another *Confusion* out of it, which is contrary to our *intention*, and only, as mentioned above, requireth a single *Materia*. *Haly* testifieth clearly to this when he saith in *Lib. Secret.*, chapter 9: It is a stone, and thou shalt not mix any other thing with it; with this the Wise work, and an all-healing power floweth from it. There shall be nothing else mixed with it, either in the whole nor in its parts.

And *Morienus* saith: This masterly skill cometh in the beginning out of a root, which extendeth later into many parts and finally returned to its source Now why have the *Philosophi* bidden us to work with the imperfect metals, since these cannot be the *Materia* of the stone? And the answer is: When the *Philosophi* order the impure bodies to be taken, they did not mean thereby copper, iron, lead, tin, etc., but they meant its *Corpus* or its earth; as *Arnoldus* in *Flore florum* saith: The *Mercurius* is added to the earth, *i. e.*, to the imperfect body. And what is more, its earth in itself, however perfect and pure it can be made by Nature, still is impure and imperfect *respectu lapidis Physici*.

And herein art excelleth Nature, for it can do what Nature cannot accomplish. But since this earth, as said, is imperfect before perfect purification and regeneration, it appeareth therefrom that it cannot as yet tinge and make perfect, and hath no more than what Nature hath bestowed upon it. But when it is regenerated it may then add much. But its impurity is obviously perceptible in our work. At first it is wholly black, and then it will be comparable to lead or antimony, after that it becometh gray, and is called *Jupiter* or tin or bismuth, and all this before it turneth white. After it is white, it is called *Mars* and *Venus* before it is brought to a complete redness. *Basilius Valentinus* is of the same opinion, and seeketh many another, as he doth set forth in the above-mentioned book, and himself doth testify in his treatise about the great stone, where he investigateth the *Materia lapidis*, and saith: That in *Sol* the gift of all three fixities is together, and therefore resisteth every power of fire; and that *Luna*, on account of its fixed Mercury doth not escape so quickly, and doth pass its *Examen*. And thus he saith finally: The archcourtesan *Venus* is clothed and dressed with superfluous color and her master's body is of pure *Tinctur* and of the same color as abideth also in the best metals, and on account of this superfluity is proven red. And since her body is leprous, the *Tinctur* hath no permanent abode in it and must at the same time disappear with her body. For where the body is consumed through death, there the soul cannot remain, it must give way and escape. Because the abode is destroyed and burned with fire, so that its place is unrecognisable, and no one may continue to dwell there. But gladly and with understanding dwelleth the soul in a formed body. The constant salt hath given the warlike *Mars* a hard, strong, and crude body, by which is proven the valor of his mind, and one cannot easily wound this war-lord, since his body is invulnerable. But if someone should say: Because *Venus* hath a constant Sulphur it must likewise, according to the teaching of *Basilius*, be united to the *Spiritus Mercurii perfecti*, and a *Tinctur* will be made therefrom. What hath already been said many times, and what hath been stated by *Basilius* himself, should be borne in mind: That our *Materia* must not be taken from many things, since the *Universal* is one thing, and can only be found and extracted from a single thing; and that the *Spiritus Mercurii* and *Anima Sulphuris* including the spiritual salts, are united together under one heaven and dwell in one body. So will he cease from his error and, without further consideration, turn his thoughts to the perfect metals, observing the saying of *Plato*, quart. 2. Why do ye calcinate and dissolve the other bodies with great difficulty, since ye can find in this (perfectly) what ye seek? But is ye ever want to use it, then it is necessary that ye first transform it into the nature of the perfect body.

Therefore, my dear seeker of the natural secrets, leave all animal and vegetable things, all salts, alum, vitriol, marcasite, magnesia, antinomy, all imperfect and impure metals, and seek for thy stone in *Mercurius* and *Sol*, for the gold, and in *Mercurius* and *Luna* for the silver, since this is the essence of the whole art, according to *Arnoldus de Villa Nova, Rosar.*, part 1, chapter 7. Just as the fire in the beginning is a sealed fire, saith *Riplaeus*, porta 1. Thus gold is also the beginning of gold-making. If, therefore, thou wouldest make gold and silver through the philosophic art, do not take for that purpose eggs or blood, but gold and silver, which engender a new birth, augmenting their kind, as do all other things when calcinated intelligently and naturally, but not through manual work. Therefore *Richardus*, chapter 10, admonisheth us: That one should sow gold and silver, that through our work an the intervention of Nature, they may bear fruit: since they have it in themselves and that is what one seeketh, and no other thing in the world. And why should one not choose both of these, since, according to *Richardus*, chapter 12, they have a pure and perfect *Mercurius* within them and a red and white Sulphur? For *Avicenna* saith that in every gold there is a red sulphur. But such sulphur is not found on the whole earth except in these two bodies. Therefore we very subtly prepare these two *Corpora*, that we may obtain the Sulphur and Mercury from such *Materia*, as gold and silver have from beneath the earth. They are luminous bodies, and coloring rays are in them, which tinge other bodies in true red and white, according to their preparation. For as *Arnoldus, Rosar.*, lib. 1, chap 5, saith: Our masterly skill aideth the perfect bodies and maketh perfect the imperfect ones, without a mixture of any other thing. Now, since gold is the noblest of all metals, so is the *Tinctur* of the redness, the coloring and transforming of every *Corpus*. But the silver is the *Tinctur* of whiteness, which coloreth all *Corpora* true white.

Now let the good-hearted reader be informed that such metals as gold and silver are not the *Materia* of our stone in their metallic form; they are the medium between them and our great stone. Hear therefore what *Bernardus Count of Trevisan* hath to say in another part of his book: They will do well to keep silent who do not produce our *Tinctur*, but another, which is not true, not plausible, and good for nothing; and let those be silent who claim that there is another sulphur than ours hidden in the belly of *Magnesia*.

And let those also be silent who want to extract an *Argentum vivum* from anything other than the *derment* or red knight, and want to extract another water other than our everlasting one which doth not mix with anything unless it be of its own nature, and doth not melt or dissolve anything unless it be of its own metallic nature. For there is no vinegar other than ours; no other management other than ours; no other *Sublimation* other than ours; no other dissolution other than ours; no other putrefaction other than ours; no other *Materia* other than ours.

Therefore renounce the alum, salts, vitriol, and all other *Arramenta*, borax, strong water, and all herbs, animals, beasts, and whatever may come from them, hair, blood, urine, human seed, flesh, eggs, and mineral stones, and every metal by itself alone. Even if the beginning of our *Materia* is from them, it should at the same time, according to all the aforesaid Philosophers, be based upon Mercury, which will be found in no other thing than metals. As appeareth from *Geber, et al.*

But still they are not our stone so long as they are in their metallic form. For it is impossible that the one, yea, the very same *Materia* should have two forms at the same time. For how could the stone, which hath a worthy and medium form, be between the metal and the Mercury, if they be not destroyed beforehand, and their metallic form hath not been taken from them? Wherefore saith *Raymundus Lullius* in chapter 56 of his *Testament*: Therefore the good artist taketh the metals as mediums in the work of masterly skill, and especially doth he take *Sol* and *Luna*, and he taketh these because they have both come to a moderate uniformity and great purity of their sulphureous and mercurial substances, and because they are boiled, pure, and well-timed through Nature's working, to which *proportion* the artist would struggle in vain if he should attempt to accomplish his purpose from the natural beginning without effective means.

And furthermore he saith in his *Codicil*: Without these two, namely gold and silver, the art cannot be brought to perfection, because in them is the purest substance of Sulphur, which Nature hath completely purified. In effecting this purification, art is much less effective than Nature, and it could never achieve it, as hard as it might try.

Our medicine can be made from these two bodies, if they are prepared with their Sulphur or *Arsenicum*, but not without them And he saith in the preface to his *Clavicule*: I advise you, O my friends, that ye work with nothing but *Sol* and *Luna*, to reduce them again to their first *Materia*; namely, into our Sulphur and Mercury. For, saith *Arnoldus*, lib. 1, *Rosar.* chapter 7, from these bodies the very white and red Sulphur will be extracted, because therein in the greatest quality is the purest sulphureous substance, cleansed by Nature to the highest degree.

Thus saith *Nicarus* in the *Turba Philosophorum*; I bid the followers (of the Art) to take the gold that they want to increase and renew, then divide the water into two parts, and take one part in such a way that the gold is concentrated in it. For the metal, when it falleth into this water, will be called the *Ferment* of the gold. But why doth the Philosopher here call the water his gold, when he saith: When the metal falleth into this water, it shall be the *Ferment* of the gold? Let this be known to my art-seeking followers: That the *Philosopher's* gold is not common gold. *Senior* saith, and it is written in the first exercise of the *Turba*: As the *Mercurius* is the origin of all metals, so also is the sun the end and last of all metals; and all metals, whether they be pure or impure, are in their innermost *Sol, Luna*, and *Mercurius*. But one is a true sun, which is extracted from it.

And therefore thou understandest that the *Philosopher's* gold, although extracted from them, is a quite different gold from the common sun or gold. So also saith the *Aurora consurgens*, chapter 16. From this it is evident that the philosophical gold is not common gold, neither in color nor in substance. For that reason it is said that it bringeth joy to the heart of man, and the same thing holdeth true with silver But what it extracted from it is a white and a red, a true, constant, and living *Tincture*. But it is the philosophical gold which one should not buy cheaply, as *Alphidius* saith. And *Morienes* saith: Everything bought dearly is deceitful. For with a very small amount of this thing and with little gold we can buy much. But in addition to that, our gold is living gold and our silver living silver, which cannot bring forth anything except life and increase. The common gold and silver are dead, which cannot accomplish anything more than is granted to them by Nature, until they are awakened by a skilled artist from their death, and obtain their life again; then they live also and can prove very effective in the increase and propagation of their kind. Concerning the death of the common metals and the life of our metals, the splendid, still living *Philosophus Michael Sendivogius*, in the 11th *Tractate* of his book about the Philosopher's Stone, speaketh thus: Thou shouldest be warned not to take common gold and silver, for they are dead: take ours, which are living. And then put them in our fire and a dry moisture will come from them. First dissolve the earth in water, called *Mercurius* by the Philosophers, and the water will dissolve these *Corpora Solis at Lunae*, so that only the tenth part remaineth with one part, and this is the deep-rooted moisture of the metals

Now to speak further about the gold of the Philosophers, it should be known that from the earliest times the *Philosophi* call their water gold, also sometimes their earth. Of the first *Modo* the *Philosophus Nicarus* hath spoken above, and the *Rosarius Philosophorum* asserts it in the following words: But what say ye to this, that the *Philosophi* say: Our gold is not a common gold, and our silver is not a common silver? To this I reply that they call water their gold, which riseth to the heights through the strength of fire; and this gold truly is no common gold. For the common man would not believe that it could rise because of its constancy.

But that the *Philosophi* also called their earth their gold is likewise attested by *Rosarius* who saith: Note that the ore is the philosopher's gold. This earth becometh ore, and is called *Ferment* and *Tincture*. Therefore saith the author who wrote *Clangor Buccinae*, in the chapter about the Solution (as also *Hermes* saith): Sow your gold in the white and leavened earth, which is made fiery, subtle, and airy through *Calcination, i.e.*, Sow so much gold, which is the soul and tingeing power, in the white earth, made white and pure by due preparation, in which is no filth.

From this is revealed that the gold of Nature is not the *Materia fermenti*, but the tingeing *Ferment is the philosopher's* gold. And thus it is written in *Scala Philosophorum*, gradu 7: Their earth wherein their gold is sown is white, and their soul is gold, and the very same *Corpus* is the place of wisdom, which it assembleth, and is the abode of the *Tincture*.

And further on the author saith: For that reason *Hercules* saith: Pour it again, *i.e.*, dissolve the body of Magnesia, which hath become white and like raspberry leaves. For that body seeketh refuge in the best, and the gold extracted from it is called the gold of the philosophers, and is a *Tincture*, hence is a soul. For with the water the *Spiritus* riseth into high air, and this white *Corpus*, when the gold hath become white, they have called our gold after our blackness. Therefore *Senior* saith: Mix gold with gold, *i. e.*, water with ashes. And *Hermes*: Sow gold in leavened earth. Therefore the *Philosophi* write that our gold is no common gold.

To this positive opinion someone might here reply and ask: Why do the philosophers sometimes conceive of their gold as water, but at other times as earth? Doth this not look as if they contradict each other and do not agree about these matters? That they confound these things? Or do they want to mislead their followers? The answer to this is that each and all of the Philosophers, where they have shown the truth, have shrouded it in hidden sayings, and therefore they do not contradict each other, but agree wonderfully with each other, as if speaking with one mouth. They do not create any confusion, and do not seek to mislead the worthy follower, but they present to him truly and clearly, in figurative language, all their secrets before his eyes, but which they conceal and darken before the unworthy and ungodly as much as the Highest God hath given them His mercy, so that such noble pearls will not be cast before swine, which follow only their bodily desires; and thus the Holy Sanctuary will not be desecrated. So in respect to the present question the Work proveth itself.

For the good-hearted follower of our art is many times sufficiently instructed, not only as to where our *Materia* should be obtained, but also that it is a single *Materia* which, through the skill of the artist, is dissolved into two things, *viz.*, into water and earth, or *Mercurium* and *Sulphur*. Now if the *Philosophi* call the water "gold" or the earth "gold," they do nothing amiss, for it is a question of their own free will how they shall name it: since they also call their stone their gold, a more than perfect gold, a regenerated gold, and many more names of the kind. But not everyone can understand their meaning, as hath to be accredited to his ignorance rather than to the ill-will of the Philosophers in writing.

And now the art-seeking follower is sufficiently and completely informed of the super-excellent secret of the *Materia* of our great stone, and that it cannot be taken out of any kind of vegetable growth, or any kind of animal, out of no kind of mineral, and out of no imperfect metal, but it must be extracted from gold and silver, and that our gold and our silver are not the common dead gold and silver, but is that of the Philosophers which is living gold and silver.

Now all that the remaineth to be done is to be instructed about the *Solution*, the greatest secret of the entire Work.

Now to speak about the *Solution*: This occureth at once if one maketh something dry moist, softeneth something hard, and revealeth something hidden, *i.e.*, when one transformeth a hard thing into water, but not into common water, as *Parmenides* and *Agadmoe* the *Philosophi* teach in the *Turba Philosophorum*, where they say: There are some who, when they hear about the dissolving of the bodies, believe it is a water of the clouds. But if they had read and understood our books, they would know that our water is permanent, especially in the water of the Philosophers, *i.e.*, in the first *Materia*, as saith *Arnoldus* in *Rosarium* 1, *chapter* 9. The work of the Philosophers is that they dissolve their stone in their Mercurium, that is, they bring it again into its first *Materia*.

And *Avicenna* saith: If thou wouldst work, then it is necessary that thou dost first start with the dissolving and *Sublimation* of the two lights, especially since this is the first step of the work, that Mercury cometh therefrom. Therefore *Arnoldus*, lib. 2, chapters 1 and 2, hath written: The *Solution* is a separating of the bodies, and preparation of the *Materia* or nature.

And *Richardus Anglicus*: The beginning of our work is to dissolve the stone into its first *Materia* and the fusion of the body and spirit, so that it becometh a mercurial water. But just as the *Solution* is the first and the most necessary part of our work, so it is also the most difficult part of it. *Eubaldus Vogelius* testifieth not badly to it when he saith: How difficult a work the preparing of the *Solution* is they know who have labored at it.

And *Bernhardus, Count of Trevisan*, writeth in his letter to *Thomas of Bononiae*: He who knoweth the art and science of the dissolving, that is, he who hath attained to the secret of the art, which is to mix the forms and extract the natures out of the natures, which lie effectively concealed therein. Then again this *Solution* must not occur with caustic waters, since all caustic waters disturb and destroy the *Corpus* which they should dissolve and perfect. And in addition, as hath already been said, no dissolving in the water which wetteth the hands is required, but rather a dry water, *i.e.*, the first *Materia*, which is not called *Mercurius* alone, but also *Sulphur*.

Concerning this *Zeumon* also speaketh in the *Turba*: Ye do work in vain unless ye grind the *Corpora*, break them, dissolve them, and govern them industriously, until ye extract their fat and make an incomprehensible spirit from it.

And thus saith *Richardus Angelicus*, on the advice of *Avicenna*: The *Philosophi* considered studiously in what form they should extract the Sulphur from the perfect bodies, and how they might better purify their qualities through their art, so that such a thing might come out of it with the aid of Nature as no one had seen in them before, and they say that this could not be done without the dissolving of the bodies and returning them to the first *Materia* could never occur, which is nothing else than the Mercury out of which they had been made before, and it is this Mercury alone, without mixture or addition of any alien matter. For our *Corpora* are not dissolved by any waters, except that of their own kind, which can be thickened by the bodies, as saith *Bernhardus* in his epistle to *Thomas of Bononiae*. And a little before in the same epistle he saith: The dissolving requireth a remaining together, namely that of the dissolving and the dissolved, that out of both the male and female seed come forth in a new form. I tell thee in all truth that no water dissolveth the metallic form through natural *Reduction* except that which remaineth with them in the *Materia* and *Forma*, and that which can again coagulate the dissolved metals.

And *Morfoleus* saith in the *Turba*: Every *Corpus* will be dissolved by the spirit with which it is mixed, and will become, undoubtedly, spiritually one with it, and each spirit will be changed and colored by the bodies, with which spirit a tingeing and the fire-withstanding color is mixed.

Now, if all this be true, then the *Discipulus*, seeking the art, hath only to reflect diligently upon what kind of water it is, since he hath to strive for the knowledge of the *Menstruum*, whose things are one, and without which nothing can be accomplished in the mastery of this art, as saith *Raymundus* in *Compendio animae*. For there is nothing in the world but our *Menstruum*, he saith in his *Codicillo*, which can join together the dissolution of the metals; since it is such a water that the metals, retaining their form, can be dissolved with it.

But while this is the great secret, which the *Philosophi* have kept most deeply hidden in their writings, but have also forbidden it to be revealed, I shall direct thee (so far as I am permitted to do so), to the right way with two philosophical dicta. The first is found in the book *Rosarii abbreviati* in the following words: The first preparation and the *Fundament* of the art is the dissolving, that is, the restoration of the body in water, *i.e.*, Mercury. And they called this the dissolving when they said: The gold, which is hidden in the body of *Magnesia*, is being dissolved, that it might be brought back into its first *Materia*, therein to become Sulphur and Mercury, not to be turned again into water, since our *Solution* is none other than the body moistened again and dissolved again into the nature of Mercury. And the salty content of its Sulphur is decreased, which holy Sulphur is extracted from two Sulphurs when the *spirit* meeteth the body.

The other dictum is to be found in *Ripley's* preface to his *Twelve Gates*: I will instruct thee in Truth that ye may understand that there are three *Mercurii*, which are the keys to knowledge, and which *Raymundus* hath called his *Menstruum*, and without which nothing can be made rightly. But two of them again differ, and are not the bodies own nature But the third is the essential *Mercurius* of *Sol* and of *Luna*, the quality of which I shall explain to thee. For the *Mercurius*, essential in the other metals, is the principal *Materia* of our stone. In Sun and Moon are our *Menstrua*, not to be seen with our eyes except through their effects

This is our stone, when some one rightly understandeth our writings. It is the soul and radiant substance of the Sun and the Moon, and the very subtle *Influentia* through which the earth receiveth its light. For what else is gold and silver, saith *Avicenna*, but the pure white and red earth? Take the abovementioned light from them and they will become earth of very little value. When everything is compounded together we call it lead. The very existence of the quality of the light originateth from the Sun and the Moon: and these are the *Summa* of our *Menstrua*.

We calcinate the perfect *Corpora* with the first according to Nature: but no impure *Corpus* will be added thereto except the one commonly called by the Philosophers the "Green Lion," which is the means for joining together the *Tinctures* between the Sun and the Moon with perfection.

With the other, which is a *vegetable* moisture, which bringeth to life that which had been dead before, both material elements as well as the formal ones, should be dissolved, otherwise they are of little value.

With the third, the tree *Hermetis* must be burned to ashes with a certainly lasting humidity, incombustible and greasy in its nature. This is our surest natural fire, our *Mercurius*, Sulphur, our pure *Tincture*, our soul, our stone, lifted up by the wind, born in the earth. Keep this well in thine heart.

This I may say to thee: That this stone is a potential vapor of the Sulphur, but thou must be careful how thou dost obtain it. For this *Menstruum* is in fact invisible, although it can still take the form and appearance of a clear water through the help of the other philosophical water, when the elements are separated.

And by very hard and strenuous work with this *Menstruum* the *Sulphur Naturae* can be made, when it hath been intensified in a natural way and hath been calcinated into a pure spirit. Then thou canst dissolve with it thy *Basis* or *Mass*.

Now these are the words of the Philosopher wherein the whole secret of the *Solution* is disclosed. Now if thou dost want to hold fast to and ponder over all the potentialities of Nature, so that thou perform all the works which Nature performeth, then thou must recall and unwind like a ball of twine, what thou wilt find herein of all truth, clearly and profoundly set forth. But if thou canst fail to note herein where the locked doors are, then thou knowest neither the *Materia* nor the power of Nature, and for this thou wilt not need any spectacles nor an imaginary *putabam*, but a most fervent prayer; and assiduous study, in addition to contemplation of the possibilities of Nature, will expedite thee.

I have acquired my knowledge solely and alone, after the revelation of the High and Great God, from the assiduous study and oft-repeated reading of good books; I do not say explicitly that I have learned about the *Materia* therein, which I could learn only from divine revelation, but what I learned confirmed and conformed thereto, also about the *Solution*, which with all Philosophers is but one, and without which neither the old nor the new Philosophers can accomplish anything. Therefore it is called also *Secretum artis* and *Arcanum Philosophorum, quod nemo nisi Deus revelare debet*, including all work, and for this I thank the Creator of all things, giving unto Him praise, honor, and glory, now and for ever. Amen.

But thou, dear reader, must have no reason to complain about me, and therefore I will reveal to thee, through the love of God, still another secret. And thou shalt know that this *Solution* although one, is divided into a *secundum prius et posterius*, as they take care to say in the schools.

The first is the dissolution of which *Arnoldus* speaketh, or the decomposition into its first *Materia*, but the other is the complete dissolving of the body and the spirit at the same time, since the dissolving and the dissolved always remain together, and together with this dissolving of the body ocurreth the *Coagulation* of the spirit. Here thou canst see quite clearly and plainly with thine own eyes all that thou dost desire to see and know: and it is only a woman's work and a child's play, because one hath so little difficulty therewith, whereof there is no need to speak further; since whoever knoweth the beginning, knoweth also how, by God's blessing, to attain the end, which, so to speak, pictureth to us all the glory, all the eternal glory, when we shall behold God in our transfigured bodies. Hence we scorn all earthly lusts and strive only for the eternal, infinite, and unspeakable delights, which, all beautiful, we shall see with our own eyes.

Herewith I shall now close this short *Treatise*, and set clearly before thine eyes, in the following parable, what is further necessary for thee to know without lack or error. And in this parable thou wilt find the whole *Practica* and if thou but follow it diligently, thou wilt arrive at the final end and true knowledge. To that end mayest thou and all of us be helped and preserved from want by God the Father, God the Son, and God the Holy Ghost, to Whom be highest praise for ever and ever. Amen.

HERE FOLLOWETH THE PARABOLA WHEREIN THE WHOLE ART IS COMPRISED

There is one thing, one in cipher and in essence,
Which Nature through art helpeth to transform
Into two, into three, four, five, as we do read.
Mercury and *Sulphur* do nourish it.
Spirit, Soul and Body, and four Elements,
The Philosopher's Stone is the fifth, which they transmit.
Without fraud shouldest thou count thy *Materia*,
A two-fold *mercurial* substance,
Free from alien Sulphur, thou shalt choose the pure
And dissolve them from the ground up entirely,
Compound them again in their true weight,
And they will lead thee unto the truth.
According to the *Solution* shalt thou soon *sublimate*,
Calcinate, and diligently *distillate*,
Coagulate, and then place it securely
In a container, then begin to tinge,
And thou hast put up a medicine
To heal men and metals — as you choose.

Once upon a time I went walking in a beautiful green and young wood and mediated upon and deplored the hardships of this life and upon how we came, through the troublesome fall of our first parents into such misery and distress. Thus thinking, I left the common path and I came, I know not how, upon a narrow footpath, very rough, untrodden, and hard to walk upon, overgrown with many bushes and shrubs, and it was easy to see that this trail was very little used. Thereupon I became frightened and wanted to turn around and go back, but it was not within my power, especially since a strong wind blew mightily behind me, so that I had to take ten steps ahead for every one I could take backwards.

Therefore I had to continue on the trail despite its roughness.

Now after I had walked for some length of time, I came to a lovely meadow, surrounded by beautiful fruitful trees, as in a circle. This meadow was called by the inhabitants *Bratum felicitatis*. There I met with a group of old men with snow-white beards save for one young man with a pointed black beard; and among them was one whose name I knew, and who was still younger, but as yet I could not see his face. And they had a great dispute about all kinds of things, especially about a high and great secret which was hidden in Nature and which God kept hidden from the great world, revealing it only to those few who loved Him.

I listened to them for a long time, and I liked their discourse very much, but some of them seemed to maunder absurdly not indeed about the *Materia* or the work in question, but about the *Parabolae Similitudes* and other *Parergons*. Therein they followed *Aristotle*, *Pliny*, and other *Figmenta*, each of whom had copied from the other. Here I could no longer contain myself, but put in mine own word, refuting many futile things out of my *Experients*, and there were many who gave heed to me, examining me in their *Faculty*, putting me through some very hard tests. But my foundation was so good that I came through with all honors, and they wondered a great deal about it, but unanimously took me into their *Collegium*, for which I was heartily glad.

But they said I could not be a real *Collega* until I first learned to know their Lion and knew fully what he could and would do internally as well as externally. Therefore I should apply myself diligently to making him submissive to myself. I was rather sure of myself, and promised them that I would do my best. For I enjoyed their company so much that I would not have parted with them for any amount of money.

They led me to the Lion and described him to me very carefully. But what I should do with the beast in the beginning no one would tell me. Some of them gave me hints thereon, but so confusedly that not one in a thousand could understand them, and after I had tied up the lion and made sure that his sharp claws and pointed teeth could not harm me, they no longer kept anything secret from me. The lion was very old, ferocious, and big, and his yellow mane hung over his neck, and he seemed unconquerable, and on account of my *Temerity* I was almost terrified, and I would gladly have turned back but for my agreement, and the old men stood all around me to see how I would begin, which also kept me. With good confidence I went up to the lion in his den, and began to cajole him, but he glared at me so intensely with his flittering eyes that out of fear I nearly let my water. At the same time I recalled having heard from an old man on our way to the lion's den that very many people had undertaken to conquer this lion, but very few had really done so. I did not want to come to grief, and I remembered many a grip I had learned through great diligence in athletics, and besides I was well versed in natural *Magia*, so that I forgot about the cajoling, and attacked the lion so fast, artfully, and subtly that I pressed the blood from his body, even out of his heart; it was beautifully red, but very choleric, and this I did before he even realised it. But I looked further into his anatomy and found many things about which I had to wonder greatly, especially his bones which were as white as snow and there were more of them than of his blood.

When my dear old men, standing around the den and watching me, became aware of what I had done they began to dispute with each other vehemently, but I could not hear what they said because I was still so deep in the den, and I could only see their gestures. But when they began to utter hard words to each other, I heard one who said: He must revive the lion also, else he cannot be our *Collega*. I did not intend to raise difficulties, left the den, went across a great square and came, I know not how, to a great wall, the height of which was over 100 ells against the clouds, but it did not have the width of a shoe, and from the beginning of the wall where I started unto the end, there ran on top of it an iron rail, well secured with many supports. On top of this wall I walked and thought I noticed someone going a few paces ahead of me on the right side of the rail.

After following that person for some time, I noticed some one following me on the other side of the rail, and I still doubted whether it were a man or a woman who called me and said it would be better to walk on his side than where I was going, and I believed it readily, for the hand-rail which thus stood in the middle made the walk very narrow and it was hard to walk on such a height. And then I saw some people behind me who wanted to go that way. Therefore I swung myself under the rail, grasping it tightly with both hands, and I continued on the other side until I came finally to a place on that wall which was dangerous to descend. Then I regretted that I had not stayed on the other side, for I could not pass under the rail again, and it was also impossible for me to turn back and take the other way again. Therefore I took a chance, trusted my good feet, held on tightly, and came down without harm. And when I had walked on for some time, I had forgotten all about danger and also did not know what became of the wall and hand-rail.

But after I had thus come down, there stood a beautiful rose-bush, on which grew beautiful white and red roses, but more red than white ones, some of which I broke off and put upon my hat. Whereupon I was aware of a wall enclosing a great garden, and in the garden were young fellows, and where the maidens would have liked to be, but who did not like to make so great an effort as to walk around that wall in order to come to the door. I was sorry for them and went back the way I had come, then upon a more level way, and I went so fast that I soon reached several houses, where I thought to find the house of the gardener. There I found many people, each of whom had his own chamber, and two were working together slowly and diligently. But each had his own work. I thought I had done all this work which they were doing before them, and I knew all their work, and I thought: Look, since so many other people do such squalid and dirty work only for the appearance of it and according to their own notion, having no *Fundament* in Nature, then thou art thyself forgiven. Therefore I did not want to remain any longer, because I knew that such art would disappear in smoke, and I continued on my planned way.

As I now went toward the garden door, some people looked at me sourly, so that I feared lest they hinder me in my *Propositio*. But others said: See, he wanteth to go into the garden, and we who for so long a time did services for the garden have never entered it. Let us jeer at him, if he doth blunder. But I did not pay attention to them, for I knew better than they the situation of the garden, although I had never been in it, and I went right up to a door that was locked tightly, where one could not find even a key-hole from outside. But I noticed a small round hole in this door which one could not see with common eyes, and I thought it was necessary to open the door there. I took out my master-key, prepared for this occasion, unlocked the door, and entered. After I was inside, I found some more locked doors, but I opened all of them without much trouble But this was a passageway, as if it were in a well-constructed house, about six shoes wide, and twenty long, covered with a ceiling And although the other doors were still locked, I could see through them sufficiently into the garden as soon as the first door was opened.

In God's Name I walked further on in the garden, and found in the midst of it a little garden, square in shape, and measuring six rods on each of its sides. It was covered with briar-rosebushes, and the roses thereon blossomed very beautifully. And since it had rained a little and the sun was shining, there was a beautiful rainbow. When I had left the little garden and had arrived at the place where I should assist the maidens, I noticed that instead of the walls there stood a low wattled fence, and a most beautiful maiden, bedecked in white satin, with a most splendid youth, went past the rose-garden, one leading the other by the arm and carrying many fragrant roses in their hands. I spoke to them and asked them: How did they come over the fence? She said: My dearest bridegroom helped me over it, and we are now going out of this lovely garden into our chamber to enjoy our friendship I said: I am pleased that you can satisfy your desire without any further effort on mine But see, how I ran so long a way in so short a time, only to serve you. After this I came to a great mill, built inside of stones. In it were not flour bins nor any other things necessary for milling, and one did not even see any waterwheels turning. I ask how all this came about, and the old miller answered me, saying that the milling-machinery was locked up on the other side, and I saw the miller's servant go in to it on the covered passage-way, and I followed him But when I stood in the passage and beheld the water-wheels on my left side, I stood still, marvelling greatly at what I saw. For now the wheels were above the passage, the water was as black as coal, and the drops therefrom were white, and the passage was not more than three fingers wide. Nevertheless I risked going back, holding on to the logs which were over the passage, and came over the water unwetted. Then I asked the old miller how many waterwheels he had. Ten, he answered. I could not forget this adventure and I would have liked to know its meaning. When I saw that the miller did not want to reveal anything, I departed, and there was in front of the mill a high paved hill, and on top of it some of the above-mentioned old men, walking in the warm sunshine, and they held a letter in their hands, written by the entire *Faculty* and addressed to them, about which they took counsel. I soon noticed what it might contain and that it might concern me, therefore I went up to them and said: Sirs, is it about me? Yes, they answered, you have to keep the wife you married a short time ago, in wedlock, or we have to report it to our Prince. I answered: This will be very easy, for I was, so to speak, almost born with her and raised together with her from childhood, and because I had once taken her, I shall keep her always, and even death itself shall not part us, for I love her with all my heart. They replied: What then have we to complain about? the bride is also happy, and we know what she doth want: ye must be joined together. I am well satisfied, I answered. Well, said one of them, then will the lion also come back to life and be mightier and more powerful than before

Then I recalled my previous exertion and work, and for some strange reason I thought that all this did not concern me, but some one whom I knew well. And thus thinking, I saw our bridegroom with his bride in their above-mentioned garments, going away, ready and prepared to be joined together, which pleased me greatly. For I had been in great fear lest these things might concern me

Now when, as said, our bridegroom in his brilliant scarlet clothes came to the old men with his beloved bride whose white satin frock radiated in very bright rays, they were both soon joined together, and I marvelled not a little that this maiden, who might still be her bridegroom's mother, was yet so young that she seemed to have been born but recently.

Now I do not know wherein these two had sinned; it may be that they, being brother and sister and bound together in such a way that they were not to be separated, had been accused of incest. Instead of a bridal bed and true marriage, they were condemned and locked up in a strong and everlasting prison, to repent and pay for their evil deeds with everlasting tears and true regret. But because of their noble birth and rank, and in order that they might not do anything secretly any more, and that they might be always before the eyes of the watchman who was ordered to take care of them, their prison was transparent, crystalline, and formed not unlike a heavenly dome. But before this, all their clothes and ornaments with which they were adorned were taken from them, so that they had to live naked and bare in their dwelling-place. And no one was given them to wait upon them. But all the food and drink which was drawn from the above-mentioned water, which was necessary for them was placed therein. The door of their chamber was well locked and sealed with the seal of the *Faculty*, and I was ordered to guard it and since winter was soon to come, to heat their chamber duly, so that they should not freeze or burn, but in such a way that they could in no wise come out and escape. But if any damage should occur under the said *Mandatum*, I would certainly receive great and severe punishment therefor. I did not feel well about this matter, and my fear and worry made me faint-hearted For I thought to myself that it was not a small work which I was commanded to do, but I knew that the *Collegium sapientiae* was not given to lying and always did what it said, and certainly prepared its work with care. However, I could not change it, and besides this locked chamber stood in the middle of a strong tower, surrounded by high walls and strong fortifications, and since one could heat the chamber with a moderate but constant fire, I undertook my office and began in God's Name to heat the chamber in order to protect the imprisoned married couple from the cold. But what happens? As soon as they notice the slightest warmth, they embrace each other so lovingly that one will not see the like again And they stay together in such ardor that the heart of the young bridegroom vanished in fervent love, and his entire body melted and fell apart in the arms of his beloved. Then she, who had loved him no less than he had loved her, saw what had happened, she shed many tears for him and buried him, so to speak, with them, so that one could not see for overflowing tears what had happened to him. But her grieving and crying lasted only for a short time, and because of her grief she did not want to live any longer, but went voluntarily to her death Ah! woe unto me! I was in fear, anguish and misery, because these two whom I was supposed to guard had been apparently dissolved entirely into water, and I saw them lying before me as dead Certain failure confronted me, and what seemed to be the worst and what I feared most, was the coming derision and ridicule, as well as the perils I should have to meet.

I spent a few days in careful thought, considering how I could help mine affairs, when I recalled how Medea had brought Aeson's dead body to life again. And I thought to myself: If Medea could do it, why should I not be able to do it? I began to think about how to proceed with it, but did not find any better way than to maintain the steady warmth until the water would recede and I could view the dead bodies of our lovers Then I hoped to escape all danger with gain and praise Therefore I continued for forty days with the warmth with which I had begun, when I noticed that the longer I did so, the more the water disappeared And I could see the dead bodies black as coal This would have happened sooner if the chamber had not been locked and sealed so tightly; but I was not permitted to enter it in any way Then I noticed quite particularly that the water rose high up toward the clouds, collected on the ceiling of the chamber, and came down again like rain; and nothing could escape, so that our bridegroom and his lovely bride lay before mine eyes dead and rotten, stinking beyond all measure Meanwhile I noticed in the chamber a rainbow in the most beautiful colors, caused by the sunshine in the moist weather which gladdened me not a little in my sorrows, and I became rather happy to see my two lovers lying before me again But no joy is so great that there is no sorrow in it; and therefore I was grieved in my joy because I saw the ones I was supposed to guard so lying before me that one could perceive no life in them But since their chamber was made from such firm and pure *Materia* and closed so tightly, I knew that the soul and spirit could not escape therefrom, but were still enclosed therein I continued with my steady warmth and heat day and night, performing my ordered duty, imagining that spirit and soul would not return to the bodies as long as the dampness lasted For they like to dwell in the damp nature And, indeed, I found this true. For I noticed in many painstaking observations that many vapors arose from the earth about eventide, through the strength of the sun, and went up high as if the sun were drawing up the water. But during the night they coagulated into a lovely and fertile dew, coming down in the morning, moistening the earth, and washing our dead bodies, which became all the more white and beautiful through such bathing and washing But the more beautiful and white they became, the more they lost of their moisture, until finally the air became so light and clear, while all the foggy and damp weather had passed, the spirit and soul of the bride could not remain any longer in the clear air and went back into the transfigured and glorified body of the queen, and as soon as the body felt them it became instantaneously alive Over this I rejoiced not a little, as you can very well imagine, especially since I saw her rise in a very costly garment, the like of which is seen by only a very small number of people on this earth, and she was adorned with a costly crown embellished with flawless diamonds, and I could see her rise and say: Hearken, children of men, and observe ye who are born from women, that the All-Highest hath the power to enthrone kings and to dethrone them. He maketh rich and poor, according to His will He slayeth and maketh to live again

And behold all this in me as a true and living example: I was great and became small; but now after I became humble I was raised to be a queen over many realms I was slain and made alive again. The great treasures of the philosophers and of the mighty have been entrusted and given to me, the poor one

Therefore was I granted the power to make the poor rich, to deal mercy to the humble, and to bring health to the sick But not yet am I like my beloved brother, the great and mighty king, who will still be recalled from the dead When he cometh he will prove my saying true

And while she thus spake, the sun shone brightly and the days became warmer and the dog-days were soon to come. And long before the wedding of our new queen there were prepared many costly robes, made out of black velvet, ash-gray colored damask, gray silk, silver-colored taffeta, snow-white satin, yea, a silver piece of exceeding beauty, embroidered with costly pearls and bedecked with gloriously clear glittering diamonds And in the same manner were prepared garments for the young king, namely of *Incarnat*, with the yellow colors of aureolin, costly fabrics, and finally a red velvet garment, embroidered, adorned, and prepared with costly rubies and carbuncles in very great quantities But the tailors who made these garments were invisible, and I marvelled greatly when I saw one coat after another, and one robe after another, being finished, since I knew that no one else besides the bridegroom and the bride had gone into the chamber. But what most astonished me was that as soon as one coat or robe was ready, the former ones disappeared before my very eyes, and I did not know whither they had vanished nor who had locked them away.

And after this costly coat was finished, there appeared the great and mighty king in all his power and glory, and there was nothing like unto him. And when he found himself locked in, he asked me in a friendly way, with gracious words, to open the door for him, so that he would be able to go out, and said it would be to mine advantage. And although I was strictly forbidden to open the chamber, I was so terrified by the great appearance and the sweet power of persuasion of the king that I opened the door willingly. And when he left he showed himself very friendly and gracious, yea humble, so that one could truly see that nothing adorns persons of noble birth so much as these virtues.

And since he had spent the dog-days in great heat, he was very thirsty, weak, and tired, and he asked me to bring him some of the running water from below under the water-wheels of the mill. This I did, and after he had drunk a great part of it eagerly, he went back into his chamber and told me to lock the door fast behind him, lest some one should disturb him or awaken him from his slumber.

There he rested for several days, and then called me to open the door. But I observed that he had become far more beautiful, full-blooded, and glorious, and he also noticed it. Whereupon he thought it must have been a marvellous and healthy water, and he ordered more of it and drank much more of it than the first time. And I resolved to build the chamber much larger. After the king had drunk of this delicious beverage, which the ignorant do not value at all, to his heart's content, he became so beautiful and glorious that in all my life I never beheld a person more glorious or more noble in behavior and character. Thereupon he led me into his kingdom and showed me all the treasure and riches of the world, so that I have to admit that not only did the queen speak the truth, but he also gave a great part of it to those who know the treasure and can describe it. There was no end of gold and precious carbuncle-stones, and the rejuvenation and restoration of the natural powers, as well as restoration of lost health and the taking away of all diseases, was a common thing there. But what was most delightful in this kingdom was that the inhabitants knew, feared, and praised their Creator, obtaining from Him their wisdom and knowledge, and finally, after this earthly joy, they obtained eternal glory. To this end may God, Father, Son, and Holy Ghost help all of us.

AMEN.

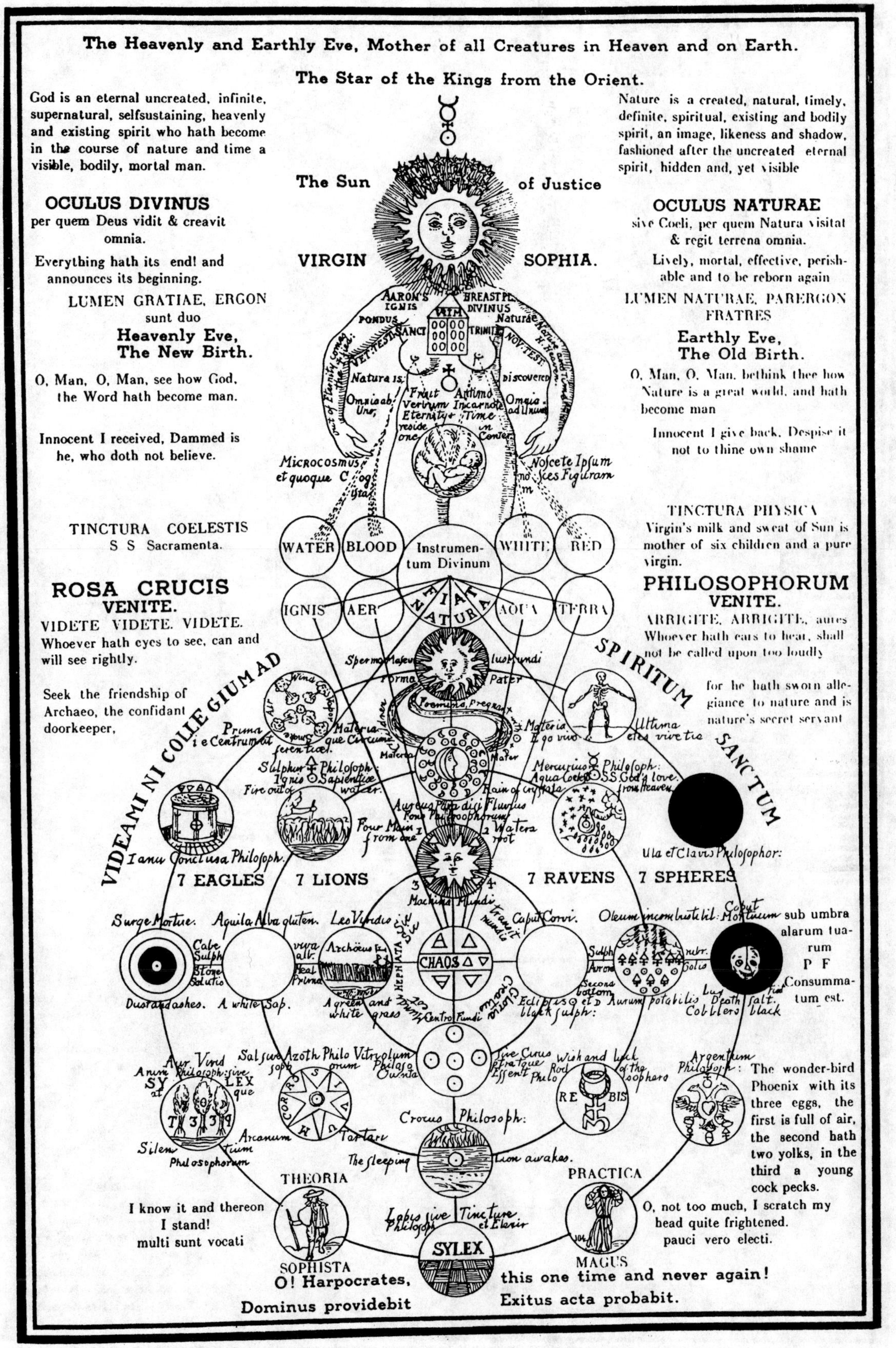
The Heavenly and Earthly Eve, Mother of all Creatures in Heaven and on Earth.
The Star of the Kings from the Orient.
God is an eternal uncreated, infinite, supernatural, selfsustaining, heavenly and existing spirit who hath become in the course of nature and time a visible, bodily, mortal man.
Nature is a created, natural, timely, definite, spiritual, existing and bodily spirit, an image, likeness and shadow, fashioned after the uncreated eternal spirit, hidden and, yet visible
The Sun
of Justice
OCULUS DIVINUS
per quem Deus vidit & creavit omnia.
OCULUS NATURAE
sive Coeli, per quem Natura visitat & regit terrena omnia.
Everything hath its end! and announces its beginning.
VIRGIN
SOPHIA.
Lively, mortal, effective, perishable and to be reborn again
LUMEN GRATIAE, ERGON
sunt duo
LUMEN NATURAE, PARERGON
FRATRES
Heavenly Eve,
The New Birth.
Earthly Eve,
The Old Birth.
O, Man, O, Man, see how God, the Word hath become man.
O, Man, O, Man, bethink thee how Nature is a great world, and hath become man
Innocent I received, Dammed is he, who doth not believe.
Innocent I give back. Despise it not to thine own shame
TINCTURA COELESTIS
S S Sacramenta.
TINCTURA PHYSICA
Virgin's milk and sweat of Sun is mother of six children and a pure virgin.
WATER
BLOOD
Instrumentum Divinum
WHITE
RED
IGNIS
AER
AQUA
TERRA
FIAT
NATURA
ROSA CRUCIS
VENITE.
VIDETE VIDETE. VIDETE.
Whoever hath eyes to see, can and will see rightly.
PHILOSOPHORUM
VENITE.
ARRIGITE, ARRIGITE, aures
Whoever hath ears to hear, shall not be called upon too loudly
Seek the friendship of Archaeo, the confidant doorkeeper,
for he hath sworn allegiance to nature and is nature's secret servant
VIDEAMINI COLLEGIUM AD
SPIRITUM SANCTUM
7 EAGLES
7 LIONS
7 RAVENS
7 SPHERES
CHAOS
sub umbra alarum tuarum
P F
Consummatum est.
The wonder-bird Phoenix with its three eggs, the first is full of air, the second hath two yolks, in the third a young cock pecks.
THEORIA
PRACTICA
I know it and thereon I stand!
multi sunt vocati
O, not too much, I scratch my head quite frightened.
pauci vero electi.
SOPHISTA
SYLEX
MAGUS
O! Harpocrates,
Dominus providebit
this one time and never again!
Exitus acta probabit.

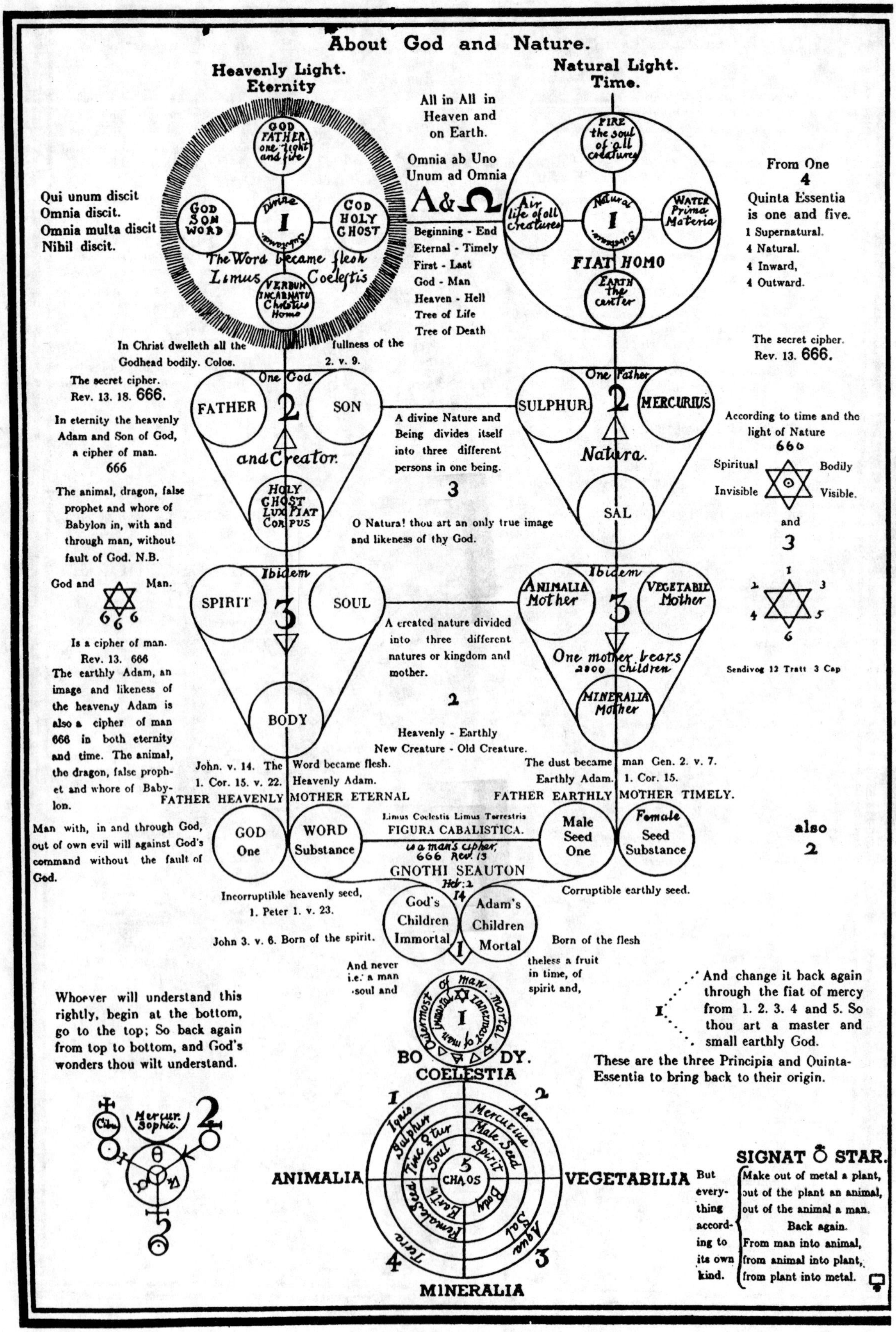
About God and Nature.
Heavenly Light.
Eternity
Natural Light.
Time.
All in All in
Heaven and
on Earth.
Omnia ab Uno
Unum ad Omnia
A & Ω
Beginning - End
Eternal - Timely
First - Last
God - Man
Heaven - Hell
Tree of Life
Tree of Death
GOD FATHER one light and fire
GOD SON WORD
Divine
I
Substance
GOD HOLY GHOST
The Word became flesh
Limus Coelestis
VERBUM INCARNATUM Christus Homo
FIRE the soul of all creatures
Air life of all creatures
Natural
I
Substance
WATER Prima Materia
FIAT HOMO
EARTH the center
Qui unum discit
Omnia discit.
Omnia multa discit
Nihil discit.
From One
4
Quinta Essentia
is one and five.
1 Supernatural.
4 Natural.
4 Inward,
4 Outward.
In Christ dwelleth all the fullness of the
Godhead bodily. Colos. 2. v. 9.
The secret cipher.
Rev. 13. 666.
The secret cipher.
Rev. 13. 18. 666.
One God
FATHER
2
SON
and Creator.
HOLY GHOST LUX FIAT CORPUS
One Father
SULPHUR
2
MERCURIUS
Natura.
SAL
In eternity the heavenly
Adam and Son of God,
a cipher of man.
666
The animal, dragon, false
prophet and whore of
Babylon in, with and
through man, without
fault of God. N.B.
A divine Nature and
Being divides itself
into three different
persons in one being.
3
O Natura! thou art an only true image
and likeness of thy God.
According to time and the
light of Nature
666
Spiritual
Bodily
Invisible
Visible.
and
3
1
2
3
4
5
6
God and
Man.
666
Is a cipher of man.
Rev. 13. 666
Ibidem
SPIRIT
3
SOUL
BODY
Ibidem
ANIMALIA Mother
3
VEGETABILE Mother
One mother bears
2000 children
MINERALIA Mother
A created nature divided
into three different
natures or kingdom and
mother.
2
Sendivog 12 Tratt 3 Cap
The earthly Adam, an
image and likeness of
the heavenly Adam is
also a cipher of man
666 in both eternity
and time. The animal,
the dragon, false proph-
et and whore of Baby-
lon.
Heavenly - Earthly
New Creature - Old Creature.
John. v. 14. The Word became flesh.
1. Cor. 15. v. 22. Heavenly Adam.
The dust became man Gen. 2. v. 7.
Earthly Adam. 1. Cor. 15.
FATHER HEAVENLY MOTHER ETERNAL
FATHER EARTHLY MOTHER TIMELY.
Man with, in and through God,
out of own evil will against God's
command without the fault of
God.
GOD One
WORD Substance
Limus Coelestis Limus Terrestris
FIGURA CABALISTICA.
is a man's cipher,
666 Rev. 13
GNOTHI SEAUTON
Heb: 2
14
Male Seed One
Female Seed Substance
also
2
Incorruptible heavenly seed,
1. Peter 1. v. 23.
Corruptible earthly seed.
God's Children Immortal
Adam's Children Mortal
1
John 3. v. 6. Born of the spirit.
Born of the flesh
And never
i.e. a man
soul and
theless a fruit
in time, of
spirit and,
Outermost of man. mortal
Innermost of man immortal
I
BO DY.
COELESTIA
And change it back again
through the fiat of mercy
from 1. 2. 3. 4 and 5. So
thou art a master and
small earthly God.
I.
These are the three Principia and Quinta-
Essentia to bring back to their origin.
Whoever will understand this
rightly, begin at the bottom,
go to the top; So back again
from top to bottom, and God's
wonders thou wilt understand.
Cibus
Mercur. Sophic.
2
1
Ignis
Sulphur
Time & tur
Soul
Aer
Mercurius
Male Seed
Spirit
5
CHAOS
Earth
Body
Female Seed
Terra
Sal
Aqua
4
3
ANIMALIA
VEGETABILIA
MINERALIA
SIGNAT ☉ STAR.
But every-thing accord-ing to its own kind.
Make out of metal a plant,
out of the plant an animal,
out of the animal a man.
Back again.
From man into animal,
from animal into plant,
from plant into metal.

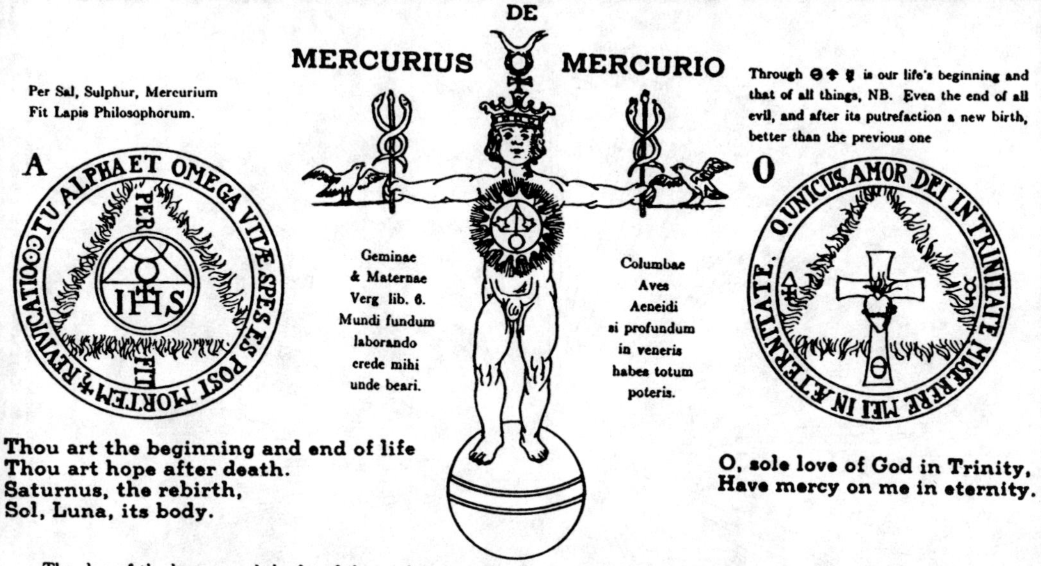

The dew of the heaven and the fat of the earth is our art-subjectum or Materia. Consequently it is neither mineral nor metal; the Pytagorean indicates to us that there are two mercurial substances of one root: Fire and water, Isch-schamaim, namely ☿, drawn out of Minera, wherein all metal and minerals are situated. It is a dew of heaven ⊖, but a mineral and metallic dew of heaven, in which are all the colors in the world, which may be coagulated through artificial operations into a sweet salt, called Manna, into a medicine; Sol pater, Luna Mater, from both these it receives its light, life and splendor, its fiery light-essence from the Sun, from the Luna its watery light-essence. We find it coagulated and dissolved. This dew falls from above into the depths of the earth and its body is made up from the most subtle parts of the earth. From above this dew receives its soul, and spirit; fire and light go into its salty body, receiving the powers of the things from above and below (nempe Virtutes Substantiales.) To our eyes appears this mineral-dew in white, yellow, green, red and black colors, these being the only colors visible to our outer eyes For it appears corporeally to the outer eyes, at times seen by miners in the mountains, appearing to the outer eye, heavy, watery, and dripping. Neither the miners nor artists know to what use to put it, since they do not know for what purpose Nature placed it there, nor of what sex it is, nor whether it be mineral or metal; all this is incomprehensible and unrecognisable. The best dew is that which in color looks like coagulated electrum or transparent amber. What the world uses it for I do not know, yet it is with all its power in all things. The dew itself is always rejected and despised; it separates into two branches, white and red, from a single-rooted , and stands upon this single root, growing like a white and red Rose of Jericho and blossoms like a lily in the valley of Josaphat, oft-times broken off untimely by miners and is tortured by ignorant workmen. The true artist knows its influence, and plucks it in full bloom, with blossom, seed, root, stem and branches, namely: In full bloom, through the faith of the inner opened eyes. This is enough said of its bodily form: It is neither metal nor mineral, but nevertheless first mother and materia of all metals and minerals.

It is nothing but a Lion with its coagulated blood, and gluten of the white eagle.

Whoever seeks it, suffer,	For He alone keeps His vow,
Whoever finds it, be silent,	Seek for friends in your mind,
Whoever holds it, hide it,	Be friendly with everybody,
Whoever may use it, do so unbeknown,	But trust no one.
Whoever is a true Philosophus,	No one but God,
Remain nameless,	If you do not want to be cheated.
Trust no one but God,	Experto crede Ruberto.

For loyalty flew from earth heavenward and left all men whose mind is upon earthly matter.

LIBER VITÆ CHRISTVS
or
The only true way to arrive at the only good and right understanding of God and nature and to attain true perfection.

ENIGMA.

Our (the right believers) dwelling-place is in a dark grey and sinister castle, bewitched, surrounded by a very thick cloud, so that no one may come near it. In front of that castle and surrounding it is a fine green lawn, on this a great rock, which hides the castle, upon the rock is a four cornered pillar, made of alabaster, on top of this stands a golden Sceptre, decked with many precious stones. Down from the rock leads a stairway made of 11 steps of white marble; around the entire edifice is a wide, deep water. On its shore lies a boat at anchor, great to look upon, bedecked with blue velvet. Its master and his servants wear crimson red mantles. Not far from it springs forth a fresh clear fountain, nearby is a pyramid and obelisk on which are written the customs of this strange island in 72 languages. If one wants to reach the princely castle, and discover it, one has first to pass through a ruined tower called the uncertain passage, from there one can view and estimate the places in the sinister and as yet invisible castle; then one comes to another tower, called the dangerous one, through which one must pass on foot, then one reaches the rock, on which the water beats, and if one touches the Sceptre thereon with the middle-finger, and conquers the wolf and a goat, which will appear suddenly, then will appear a very beautiful virgin, who will give the victor a wreath, signifying his virtue and bravery. And the clouds will part, soon the castle will be seen, and the master of the castle, in a long silken yellow coat and deep brown beret, will receive the new guest and lead him unto all earthly and heavenly happiness.

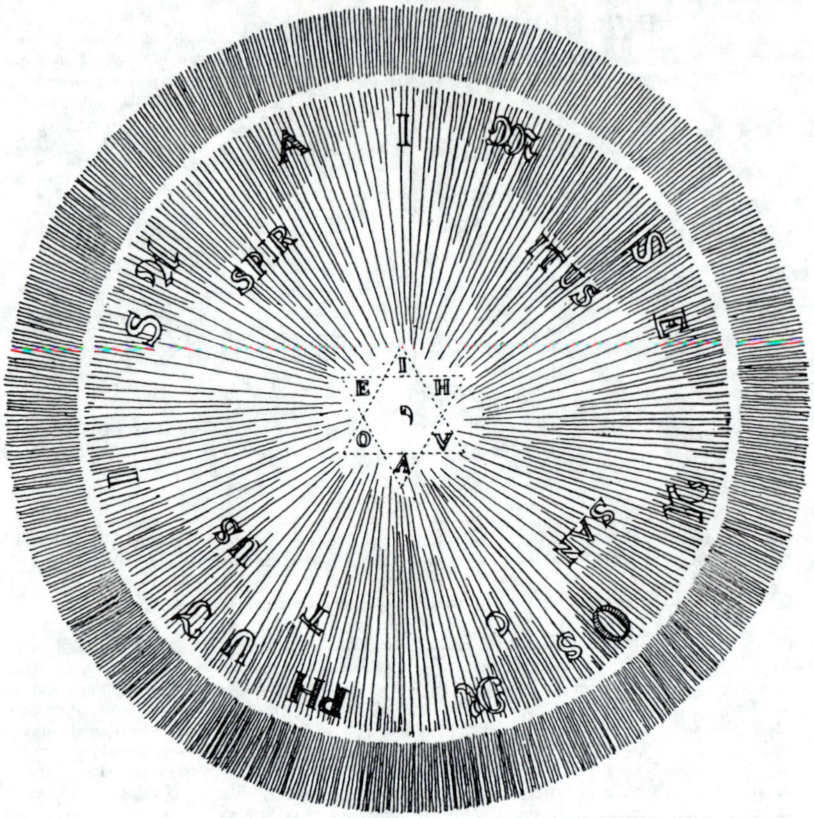

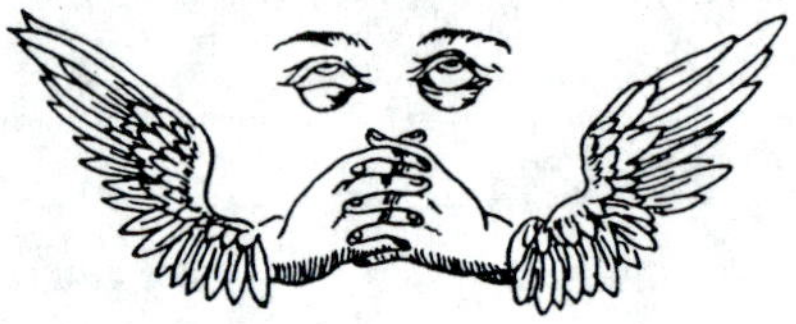

Lord from Thy hands cometh all good. All blessings and all benedictions come from Thy hand. With Thy fingers Thou hast written the character of Nature which none may read unless he be taught in Thy school. Therefore let us lift up our eyes to Thee, O Lord, even as servants look upon the hands of their master and as maids look upon the hands of their mistress, that Thou mayest help us. O Lord our God, who should not praise Thee, who should not glorify Thee, the King of Glory! For all things come from Thee and hearken unto Thee, and must all return to Thee again, being received either in Thy love or Thy wrath. Nothing can escape Thee, all things must serve Thy honor and glory. Thou alone and none other art the Lord. Thou dost what Thou wilt with Thy mighty arm, nothing can escape Thee. Thou alone dost help the humble, the meek and the poor, those who are devoted to Thee with all their heart, in their hour of need, those who humble themselves in the dust before Thee, to them Thou art gracious. Who should not praise Thee, O Thou King of Glory; there is none like unto Thee, whose dwelling place is in heaven and in a troubled and virtuous holy heart. O Great God; Thou all in all! O Nature! thou everything from nothing, what more then shall I say? I am nothing in myself, I am everything in thee, and I live in thine everything from nothing: live Thou then in me, and so bring me unto the all in Thee. Amen

ABOUT THE REVELATION OF JESUS CHRIST.

Dear Christian brethren: As Jesus Christ, the Son of God will be revealed by the Holy Ghost through His Father and the Father was revealed through His Son, so it will come to pass that those who are seemingly Christians will become Christians and all the people will accept the Christian belief and will become Christian men. But so far, as one can easily see, Jesus Christ and Christianity have never been revealed, for until now love towards the neighbor and towards God hath been entirely closed up and hath been extinguished and instead of it, rules the Flesh; i.e. idolatry, whoring, drinking, eating, envy, wrath, contention, dissension, murder, robbery, injustice and all luxury and ambition, all this being contrary to the Revelation of Jesus Christ and His bodily rebirth. Woe upon us, wretched men, that we are so much opposed to one another! Why do we fight each other with claws and teeth, is it that the love poured out by the Holy Ghost is entirely extinguished and dead? Does no one no longer respect the other man? Are we like the dumb beasts that one hath to rend, devour and destroy the other, was heaven and the earth made for one man alone? Nay, that cannot be

O, ye nobles, counts and knights, do we have to pray to God, our Creator, for the revelation and knowledge of Jesus Christ, His Son, who is despised and ridiculed, and who is nevertheless the greatest in heaven and on earth?

O, ye Theologians, Preachers including all Teachers: Ye should be taught by God and ye should proclaim Jesus Christ of Nazareth, the Crucified, to all people with right knowledge and teaching and should do so out of love and not for money or motives of profit. It is also necessary for you to ask Almighty God for the revelation and right knowledge of Jesus Christ, the Son of God and the Virgin. So then you may go ahead as the true lights of this world, before men as you have your illumination from God. Learn to know Jesus Christ, who hath made us for wisdom, for justice, for holiness, and for salvation, so that as it is written: He that glorieth, let him glory in the Lord. 1. Cor. 1. v. 31. So there will soon cease fighting, quarreling, damnation and heresy and there will be only brotherly love and unity amongst you, with the friendliness of one mind, one will, one knowledge, one belief, one blessedness and a perfect love towards neighbor and God.

O, all ye people in this world, rich and poor, man and woman, young and old, great and small, let us pray God for the revelation and true knowledge of His Son, Jesus Christ, that we may live in unity, peace, friendship, patience, kindness, and humbleness of heart, that all men in this entire world may live as of one heart, one love, one community, one church, one faith and in one mind in Jesus Christ in whom we and all men shall be blessed.

Otherwise we do not know Jesus Christ, who died for us on the cross, and no one should glorify Him with his mouth only, for He looketh into the heart, and where there is love, injustice will cease from all things, which are done in all the world.

O, ye people, loving lovingly, love of all loves, how easy is thy yoke and how light is thy burden! Thus speaketh the heavenly and eternal Wisdom and Love Itself. Matth. 11. John 3.

Eat, my Beloved, **Drink, my Friends,**
Become **intoxicated.** Cant. 5. v. 1.

Taste and see how friendly **is the Lord and think of Me,**
for My Body is the right food **and My Blood the right drink.**

Whosoever eateth My Body **and drinketh My Blood**
Abideth in Me **and I in him.**

That is how the food
affecteth what is imperishable but abideth there unto life eternal.

For the Spirit is life-giving, and **the flesh of no use, these my words**
are spirit **and life.**

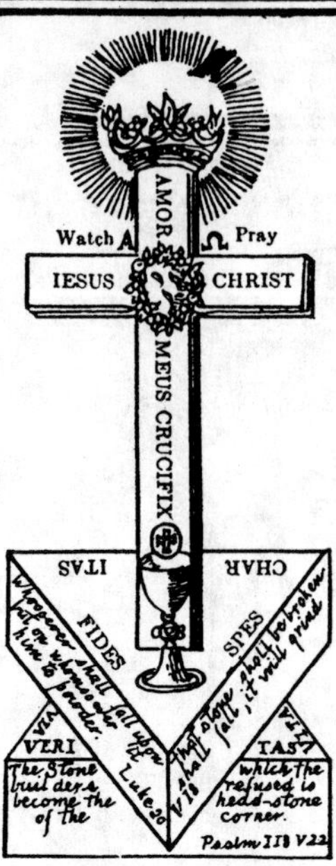

Taulerus.

The true supper is the essential, powerful and al mighty presence of Jesus Christ, the Son of the living God.

God is light and in Him is no darkness at all. But if we walk in the light as He is in the light, we have fellowship with one another, and the blood of Jesus Christ, His Son cleanseth us from all sin. 1 John 1. v. 7.

Taulerus.

Whenever God wants to give us the sweet savour of His love and kindness, He Himself becomes food and drink of our souls.

For our sins was He wounded and **through His wounds we were healed.**

EGREDERE.
per Viam **CRUCIS.**

INGREDERE.
per Vitam **LUCIS.**

To him that overcometh, will I give to eat of the hidden Manna, and will give him a white stone, and in the stone a new name written, which no man knoweth saving he that receiveth it. Rev. 2. v. 17.

Christ is the trunk and tree of life through which the bitter water of Mara was sweetened, and what are we but His twigs and branches, through which He bears fruit in us by His power. All those made white in the bitterness of this time limited life were reborn through Him into the sweeteness of eternal life.

His soul is the essential thing in my soul, and for that Soul's sake God hath become man, that we may become God-like in and through Him in the love and life of Jesus Christ. So that we may be reborn and revealed in the eternal heavenly image into a divine life. O Man: It is a great unfathomed Secret when we come to consider it and remember that we are in Christ members of one body and all of us are in Him but One. That all of us receive and benefit from the One Christ and that we are and remain in the same Christ a unified body, which body is He Himself. And we are the body and the members thereof. Yes, we are tied and bound together with and in Him to One Man, and this Man is each severally in Christ. Through the medium of bread and wine we all eat and drink Christ's body and blood with the Essential desire and desirous believing mouth, the fiery love aud life mouth of our souls. The real innermost man, a creature of paradise and of eternity, an image of God, is hidden under the gross animal form, and desires a spiritual nutriment or Tinctur and therefore eats Christ's spiritual flesh and blood, for he is a spiritual being.

The soul's hunger for the true belief is the divine spiritual mouth, eating and drinking, in the innermost depths of the soul, Christ's Body and Blood. Whatever cometh from the Spirit and consists of the Spirit that is the greatest and highest nutriment of the souls. The spiritual hungry fire of the soul reaches for, grasps, eats and drinks with its spiritual, opened, believing mouth the holy inconceivable being, Christ's Flesh and Blood. It takes this supernatural holy essential power through the medium of bread and wine, through which medium the invisible eternal becomes one with the visible, spiritual, immortal eternal human being; understand: Faith becomes through this transformation a being, a spiritual flesh and blood. For one faith can grasp the other: The earnest faith of the living grasps for the eternal: And is so mighty and powerful that it can overthrow the mountains and move them elsewhere. The true and essential faith of man is Christ Himself, who is in him and abideth in him and is his life and light. Behold, this is the way we are being purified through the faith and enlightened and inspired through the Holy Ghost. The gross animal, which is only the outer shell, receiveth only an elemental being or earthly food and eats of the perishable world-being out of which he himself consists. But the soul is of God and of His words. Mark: As is the mouth, so is also the food: Every Principium eats and drinks of its likeness: Every spirit eats and drinks of that from which it came forth, and in whose depths or Centrum it standeth: For what hath light in common with darkness? It cannot comprehend it.

The natural, mortal and perishable body receives its food from the earth; and the sidereal, volatile and perishable body its food from the firmament; but the Spirit of the Lord is the life of souls and the life of the innermost immortal life.

The innermost man as the pure Adamic power-body, with his beautiful, chosen, gracious, heavenly bride, receives in great love, desire in his spiritual believing mouth the invisible spirtual being and supernatural heavenly flesh of Christ, a tincture of life, a perpetrating fiery love and power being, for faith is the cornerstone, the beginner and the finisher, effecting, the right innermost, eternal Sabbath in the innermost depths of our souls, effecting, also, the power of God through the love of Jesus in quiet tranquility and peaceful bliss.

Christ hath not given unto His disciples the creaturely being, the outer understandable fleshly human nature, nay: Whosoever discerneth not the body of the Lord and eateth and drinketh the bread and wine, receiveth Him unto his condemnation. He gave them the spiritual human nature, the power of His body and blood, a holy, heavenly body life and loveliness, a spiritual being a spiritual body. This He brought down from heaven in which is understood the divine and eternal human power: This He introduceth into our body, made white by the light, so that He maketh us live again through His heavenly existence in our bodies.

No mortal creature can look upon a spiritual being, much less can we grasp, handle and enjoy it with our earthly mortal mouth. But such is conceivable and comprehensible to the spirit of the souls standing in the divine Centro, for He, Christ, is the body of the spirit and the spirit of the body, in our soul's body which He giveth unto us to eat in faith. No mortal and unworthy man can reach and receive the unchangeable and indescribable heavenly bread of eternity, much less can he taste of it.

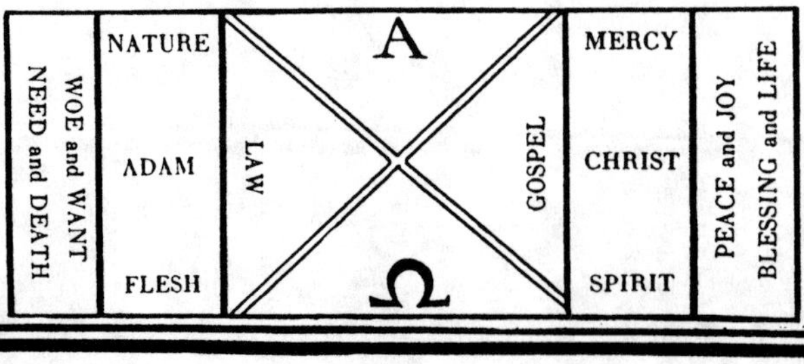

This is the revelation and the testimony and the true knowledge of J.C., God and Man, the living Book of Life, all heavenly and earthly wisdom in heaven and on earth, the sealed book according to time and eternity. And I saw on the right hand of Him that sat on the throne, a book written within and on the backside, sealed with seven seals. And I saw a strong angel proclaiming with a loud voice, who is worthy to open the book, and to loose the seals thereof? And no man in heaven, nor in earth, neither under the earth, was able to open the book, neither to look thereon. And I wept much, because no man was found worthy to open and read the book, neither to look thereon. Rev. 5. And he said unto me, these sayings are faithful and true, to shew unto his servants the things which must shortly be done. Seal not the sayings of the prophecy of this book: for the time is at hand. Rev. 22. v. 6. 10. Blessed is he whose name is written in the book of life. And I will not blot out his name out of the living book of the lamb. Philip. 4 v. 3. Rev. 3. v. 5. Rev. 21. v. 27. And whosoever was not found written in the book of life was cast into the lake of fire. Rev. 20. v. 15. Behold, I come quickly: Blessed is he that keepeth the sayings of the prophecy of this book. Rev. 22. v. 7.

The Sealed Book.

Rev. 5.

The four bands tied together, i.e., Alpha and Omega, Eternity and Time, and the one wheel to look upon not unlike four wheels, and all four were one like the other, as being one wheel in the other. So are the four beasts Ezek. 1. and the four beasts Rev. 4. 5. & 19 and the foursquare city of God fashioned after the measure of a man. Rev. 21.

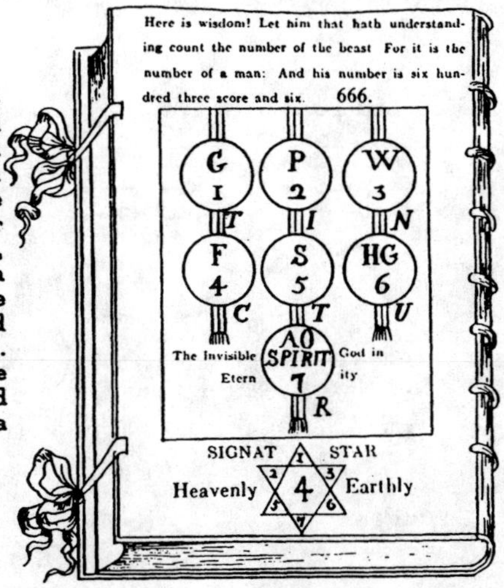

And behold: in the midst of the throne stood a lamb as it was slain and had seven horns and seven eyes, these are the 7 spirits of God, sent into all countries. i.e.,

The Seven Seals.

And I beheld a beast coming up out of the earth; and he had two horns, like a lamb and he spake as a dragon: and he exerciseth all the power of the first beast; and he causeth all to receive a mark in their right hand, or in their foreheads, that no man might buy or sell, save he that had the mark, or the name of the beast, or the number of his name: i. e. 666.

Here is wisdom, for it is the number of a man. Rev 13

All	1. Wisdom	in one	book	is and is called
	2. Power	in one	stone	
	3. Beauty	in one	flower	
	4. Riches	in one	treasure	
	5. Blessedness	in one	estate	

IESUS CHRISTUS

a † *ω*

Crucifixus & Resuscitatus.

That is:
The well, the tree, the light and the right book of life and of the lamb, he who hath that,
Understandeth all things in heaven, on earth and under the earth, and cometh forth therefrom, and all other books bear testimony thereof alone.

This is the revelation and testimony and the true knowledge of J.C., G and M, the living book of life, all heavenly and earthly wisdom in heaven and on earth, the opened book according to the Word and His holy mortal existence in the world and in time, which God hath given unto his servants. And I saw a mighty angel come down from heaven clothed with a cloud and he had in his right hand a little book open, and I heard a voice from heaven saying unto me: go and take the little book which is open in the hand of the angel, and the voice spake again and said: Take it and eat it up; and as soon as I had eaten it my belly was bitter. And he said unto me: Thou must prophesy again before many peoples, and nations, and tongues, and kings. Rev. 10. And another book was opened, which is the book of life. Rev. 20. And one of the elders saith unto me: Weep not, behold, the Lion of the tribe of Judah, the Root of David, hath prevailed to open the book, and to loose the seven seals thereof; and he came and took the book out of the right hand of him that sat upon the throne. And when he had taken the book, the four beasts and four and twenty elders fell down before the Lamb and spake: Thou art worthy to take the book and to open the seals thereof. Rev. 5. He that hath an ear, let him hear what the Spirit saith unto the churches. Rev. 2. & 3. He that hath an ear, let him hear, here is wisdom Rev. 13.

The opened book with it's seven seals.
Rev. 10.

**The 1st Band.
The Lamb with both it's horns, i.e., the heavenly and earthly kingdom according to the paternoster, and Rev. 13.**

**The 2nd Band.
Both natures united, the Godhead and Humanity in the one person of J.C.**

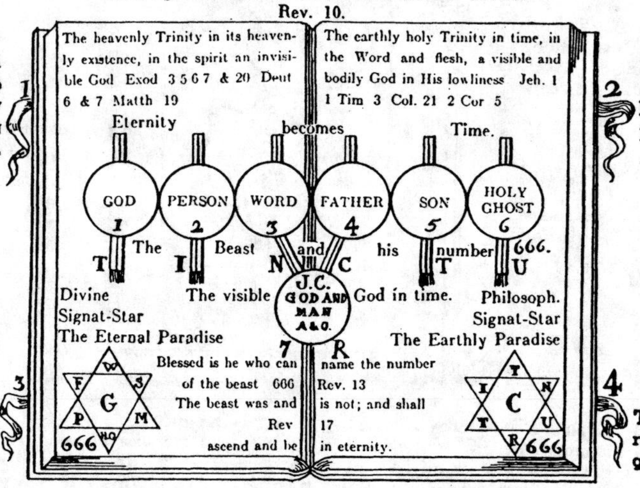

**The 3rd Band.
The old birth, the old Testament, the burning, zealous law. Exod. 20.**

**The 4th Band.
The new birth, the new Testament, the gracious Gospel.**

Close the book again with it's seven seals opened, that it may become again the first sealed book, heavenly in the invisible God. And the Spirit moveth in God, and the Person in the Son and the Father in the Word, and thus is sealed the Holy Trinity of the three heavenly, spiritual, invisible, eternal Persons united in the earthly, temporal, visible, bodily Trinity of the One Person and Mankind J.C., G. and M. And His Mortal Being is a throne, seat, heaven, house and dwelling-place is the undivided eternal Trinity, entirely in heaven and on earth, and that is the sealed book, the revelation, the true knowledge and testimony of J. C., G. and M. For in Him dwelleth the fulness of the Godhead bodily, as the holy wisdom saith. John 9. 10 12. 14. & 17. and Colos. 2.

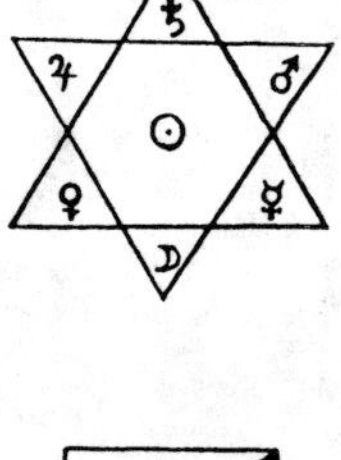

JESUS CHRISTUS

i. e.
Signat-Star.
Candles.

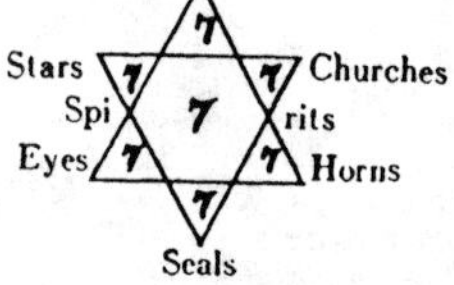

Rev. 1. 2. 3. 4. 5.

**the foundation and living corner-stone in Sion
for to see out of the depth of the spirit and truth, means
LIFE ETERNAL,
and
TO LOVE FROM THE HEART
JESUM
is better by far
than to know all things.**

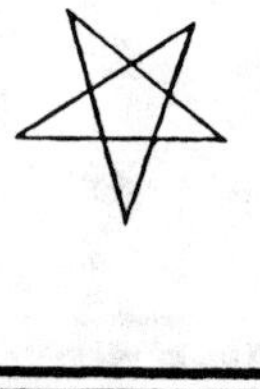

Summa Summarum: This is the final conclusion: Hidden in these two proverbs is everything within the heavenly and earthly light, and he that rightly understandeth these proverbs in eternity and time is a right and true Theosophus, Cabalist, Magus and Philosophus and he that knoweth how to interpret these two proverbs according to the Alpha and Omega is a man well to be trusted and believed. And also thou canst test anybody who can thus do this, and weigh him on the R. C. scale.

Mark this well!

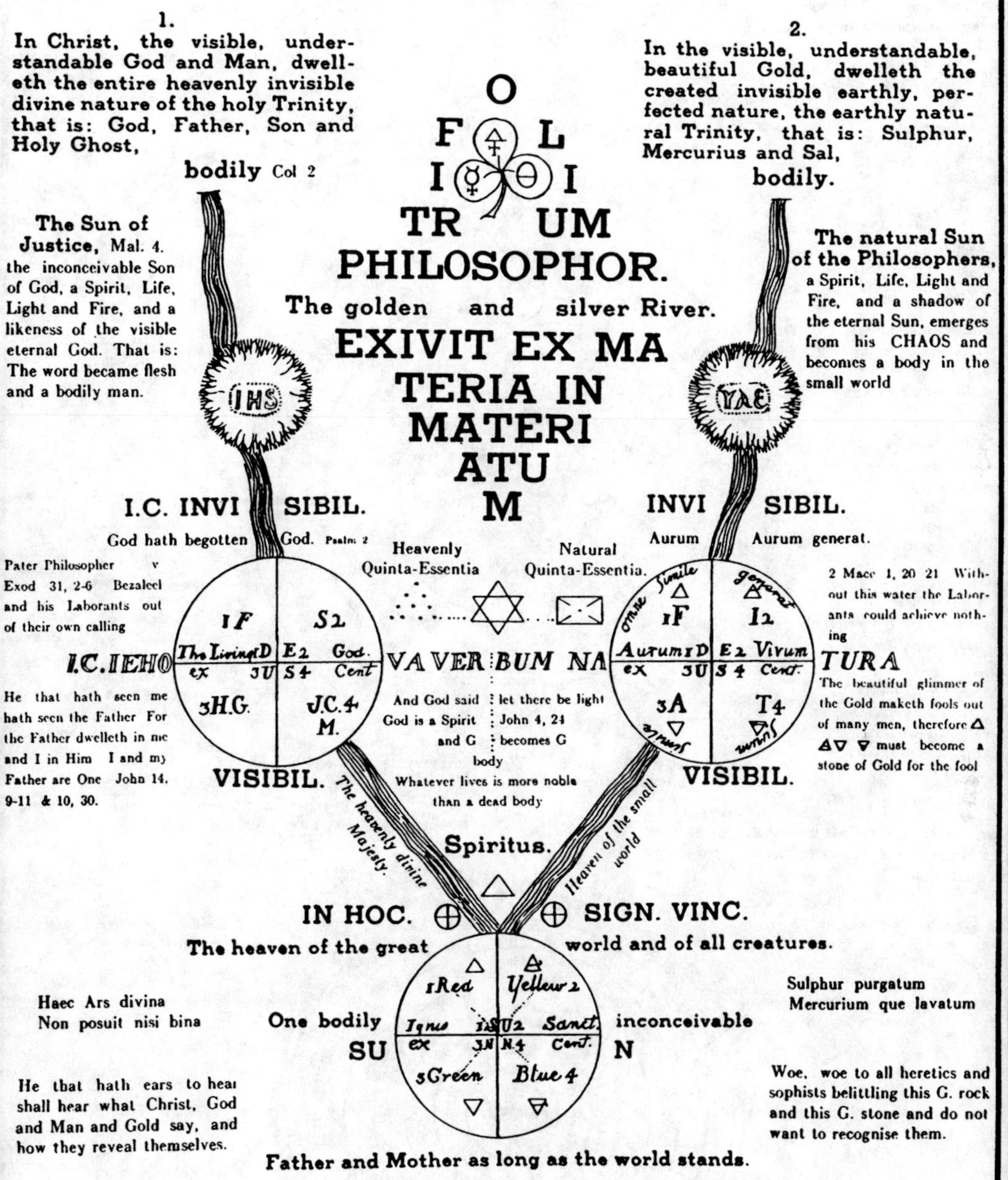

O! Fili chare, noli nimis alte volare
Si nimis alte volas, poteris comburere pennas.

Let this be a warning to those that always want to be Know-alls.

O Man, how long wilt thou lack Knowledge, how long wilt thou not even Know Thyself?

FIGURA CABALISTICA

of the Wonderful Cipher
1. 2. 3. 4.

Fire and light were the beginning. Gen 1 v 3.
Fire will be the end. 2. Pet. 3 v. 10 12.
I am Nature's palace and cottage.
Defy him that speaketh against me.

Fire and light were. 2. Cor. 4.v 6.
Fire and light will be. 1.Tim. 6.v. 16. 1. John. 1. v. 6.7.
The philosopher's Sun for him who beholdeth.
My power is in and above the earth

The Heavenly Sun
with his rainbow and 4 colours.
NATURA.

1. *the red colour*
2. *the yellow colour*
3. *the green colour*
4. *the purple colour*

☉ and ☽
have to be darkened
and have to become
black.
Mortificatio.

1. *Straight natural fire*
2. *Supernatural fire*
3. *Fire against nature*
4. *Unnatural fire*

Nature hath to work in
through itself in
The right way thou shalt
the natural and

The Earthly Sun
with his rainbow and 4 colours.
TINCTURA.

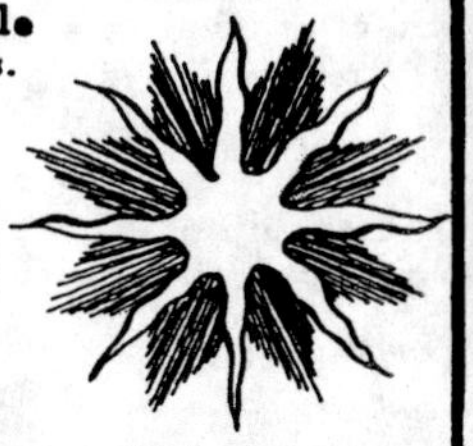

black colour 1.
green colour 2.
white colour 3.
red colour 4.

About the natural and supernatural fire.

The invisible and visible fire of the 4 Elements.

The inconceivable in the / **divine fiery light innermost**

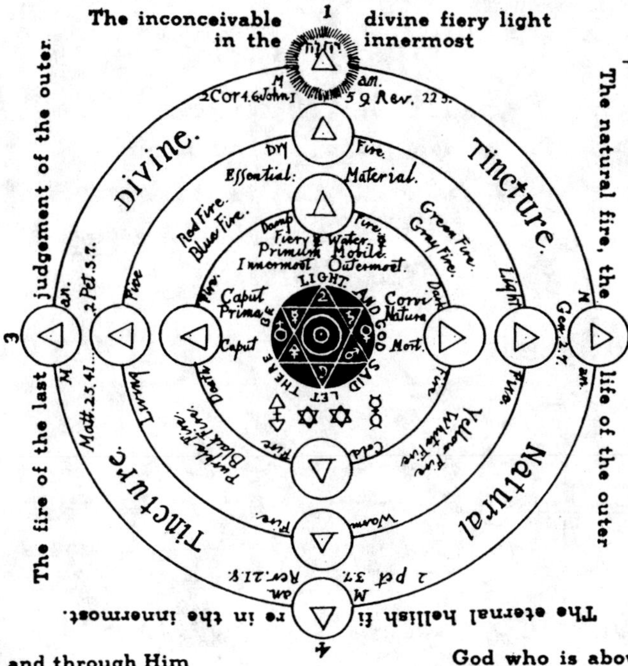

Chaos
Sperma

The preliminary work — dry way
Solve & — Coagula
Corruptio — regeneratio
Subsequent work — wet way

itself, out of itself and
a natural way.
go, will lead thee to
spiritual life.

Rom. 11 v. 36. **Of Him and through Him and to Him are all things.** Act. 17. v. 28. **In Him we live and move and have our being.**

God who is above all and through all and in you all. Ephes. 4. v. 6.

God is all in all. 1. Cor. 12. v 28 **In eternity and time,**
in heaven and the hell.

What help are Sun, Moon, Fire and Light, when man will not see, while traveling the
right way and lets a will o' the wisp lead him astray.

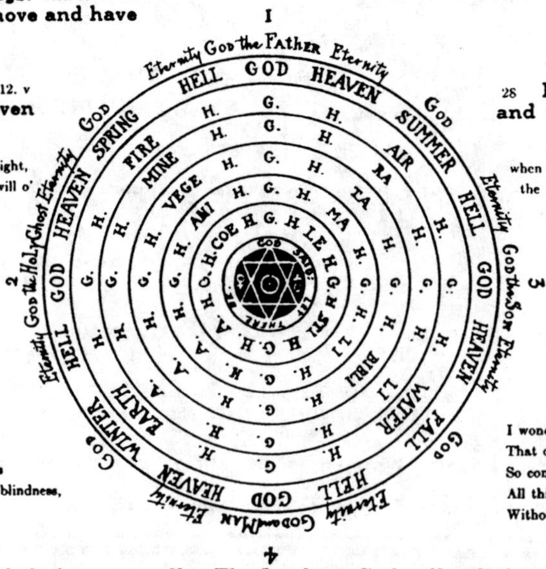

O God, how deep in darkness
Everywhere is the world!
How deep is the world in foolishness
And how is the world afflicted with blindness,
The right way is also poor.

I wonder how one goes astray,
That one cannot find reason in Nature,
So consumate are Nature's works;
All this is done through God's grace alone,
Without it all is vain.

For the Lord wilt light my candle: The Lord my God will enlighten my darkness.
Psalms. 18. v. 28.

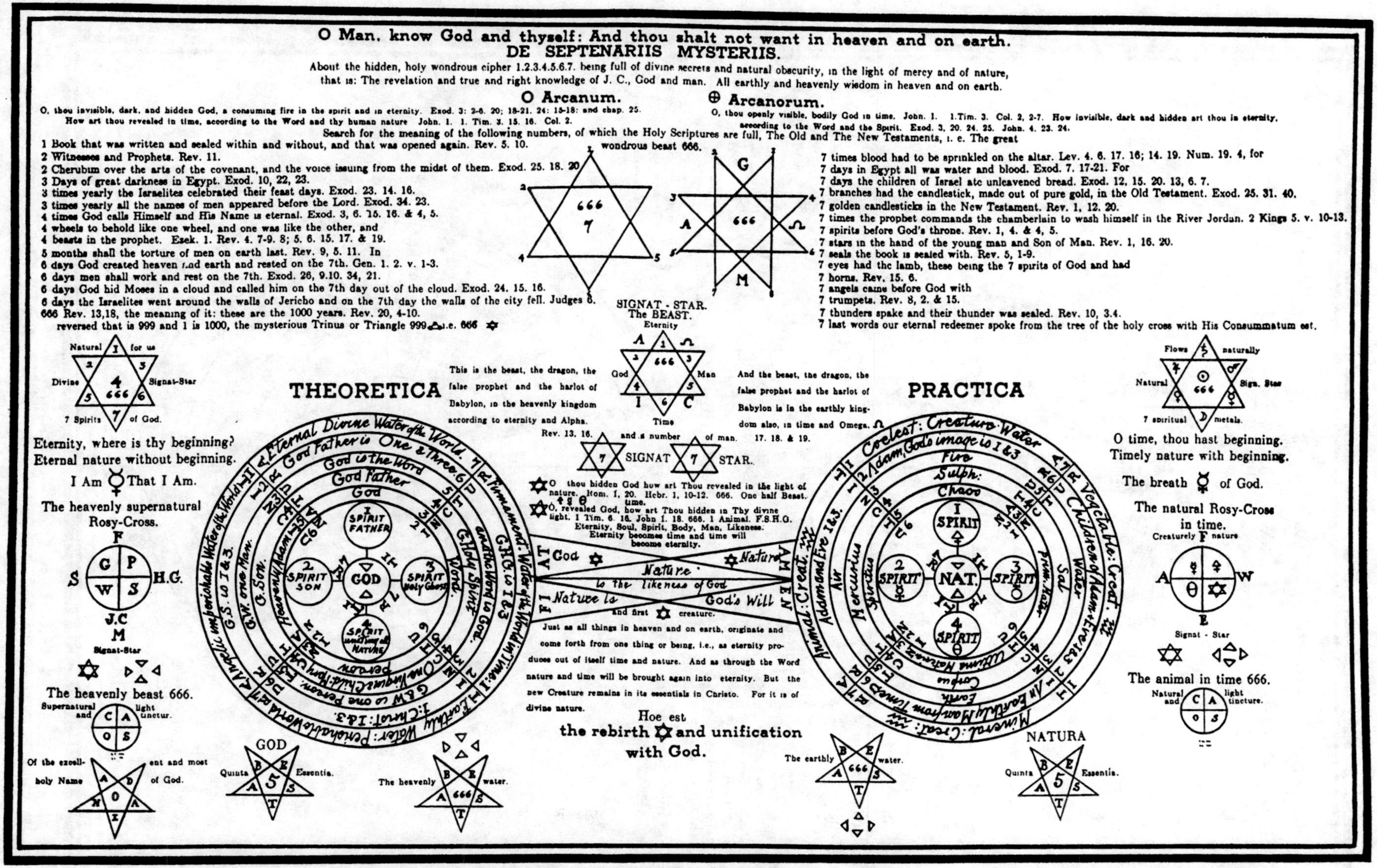
O Man, know God and thyself: And thou shalt not want in heaven and on earth.
DE SEPTENARIIS MYSTERIIS.
About the hidden, holy wondrous cipher 1.2.3.4.5.6.7. being full of divine secrets and natural obscurity, in the light of mercy and of nature,
that is: The revelation and true and right knowledge of J. C., God and man. All earthly and heavenly wisdom in heaven and on earth.
O Arcanum.
O, thou invisible, dark, and hidden God, a consuming fire in the spirit and in eternity. Exod. 3: 2-6. 20; 18-21. 24: 15-18: and chap. 25.
How art thou revealed in time, according to the Word and thy human nature John. 1. 1. Tim. 3. 15. 16. Col. 2.
⊕ Arcanorum.
O, thou openly visible, bodily God in time. John. 1. 1.Tim. 3. Col. 2, 2-7. How invisible, dark and hidden art thou in eternity,
according to the Word and the Spirit. Exod. 3, 20. 24. 25. John. 4. 23. 24.
Search for the meaning of the following numbers, of which the Holy Scriptures are full, The Old and The New Testaments, i. e. The great
wondrous beast 666.
1 Book that was written and sealed within and without, and that was opened again. Rev. 5. 10.
2 Witnesses and Prophets. Rev. 11.
2 Cherubim over the arts of the covenant, and the voice issuing from the midst of them. Exod. 25. 18. 20
3 Days of great darkness in Egypt. Exod. 10, 22, 23.
3 times yearly the Israelites celebrated their feast days. Exod. 23. 14. 16.
3 times yearly all the names of men appeared before the Lord. Exod. 34. 23.
4 times God calls Himself and His Name is eternal. Exod. 3, 6. 15. 16. & 4, 5.
4 wheels to behold like one wheel, and one was like the other, and
4 beasts in the prophet. Ezek. 1. Rev. 4. 7-9. 8; 5. 6. 15. 17. & 19.
5 months shall the torture of men on earth last. Rev. 9, 5. 11. In
6 days God created heaven and earth and rested on the 7th. Gen. 1. 2. v. 1-3.
6 days men shall work and rest on the 7th. Exod. 26, 9.10. 34, 21.
6 days God hid Moses in a cloud and called him on the 7th day out of the cloud. Exod. 24. 15. 16.
6 days the Israelites went around the walls of Jericho and on the 7th day the walls of the city fell. Judges 6.
666 Rev. 13,18, the meaning of it: these are the 1000 years. Rev. 20, 4-10.
reversed that is 999 and 1 is 1000, the mysterious Trinus or Triangle 999 i.e. 666
666
7
G
A
666
M
7 times blood had to be sprinkled on the altar. Lev. 4. 6. 17. 16; 14. 19. Num. 19. 4, for
7 days in Egypt all was water and blood. Exod. 7. 17-21. For
7 days the children of Israel ate unleavened bread. Exod. 12, 15. 20. 13, 6. 7.
7 branches had the candlestick, made out of pure gold, in the Old Testament. Exod. 25. 31. 40.
7 golden candlesticks in the New Testament. Rev. 1, 12. 20.
7 times the prophet commands the chamberlain to wash himself in the River Jordan. 2 Kings 5. v. 10-13.
7 spirits before God's throne. Rev. 1, 4. & 4, 5.
7 stars in the hand of the young man and Son of Man. Rev. 1, 16. 20.
7 seals the book is sealed with. Rev. 5, 1-9.
7 eyes had the lamb, these being the 7 spirits of God and had
7 horns. Rev. 15. 6.
7 angels came before God with
7 trumpets. Rev. 8, 2. & 15.
7 thunders spake and their thunder was sealed. Rev. 10, 3.4.
7 last words our eternal redeemer spoke from the tree of the holy cross with His Consummatum est.
Natural
for us
Divine
Signat-Star
4
666
7 Spirits
of God.
Eternity, where is thy beginning?
Eternal nature without beginning.
I Am ☿ That I Am.
The heavenly supernatural
Rosy-Cross.
F
G
P
S
H.G.
W
S
J.C
M
Signat-Star
The heavenly beast 666.
Supernatural and
light tinctur.
C
A
O
S
Of the excell-
ent and most
holy Name
of God.
THEORETICA
This is the beast, the dragon, the false prophet and the harlot of Babylon, in the heavenly kingdom according to eternity and Alpha.
Rev. 13. 16.
SIGNAT - STAR.
The BEAST.
Eternity
God
666
Man
Time
and a number
of man.
And the beast, the dragon, the false prophet and the harlot of Babylon is in the earthly kingdom also, in time and Omega.
17. 18. & 19.
SIGNAT
STAR.
PRACTICA
O thou hidden God how art Thou revealed in the light of nature. Rom. 1, 20. Hebr. 1, 10-12. 666. One half Beast. time.
O, revealed God, how art Thou hidden in Thy divine light. 1 Tim. 6. 16. John 1. 18. 666. 1 Animal. F.S.H.G. Eternity, Soul, Spirit, Body, Man, Likeness.
Eternity becomes time and time will become eternity.
FIAT
God
Nature
Nature
to the likeness of God
Nature is
God's Will
AMEN
and first
creature.
Just as all things in heaven and on earth, originate and come forth from one thing or being, i.e., as eternity produces out of itself time and nature. And as through the Word nature and time will be brought again into eternity. But the new Creature remains in its essentials in Christo. For it is of divine nature.
Hoc est
the rebirth and unification
with God.
SPIRIT FATHER
SPIRIT SON
GOD
SPIRIT Holy Ghost
SPIRIT NATURE
SPIRIT
NAT.
GOD
Quinta
5
Essentia.
The heavenly
666
water.
The earthly
666
water.
NATURA
Quinta
5
Essentia.
Flows
naturally
Natural
666
Sign. Star
7 spiritual
metals.
O time, thou hast beginning.
Timely nature with beginning.
The breath ☿ of God.
The natural Rosy-Cross
in time.
Creaturely F nature
A
W
E
Signat - Star
The animal in time 666.
Natural and
light tincture.
C
A
O
S

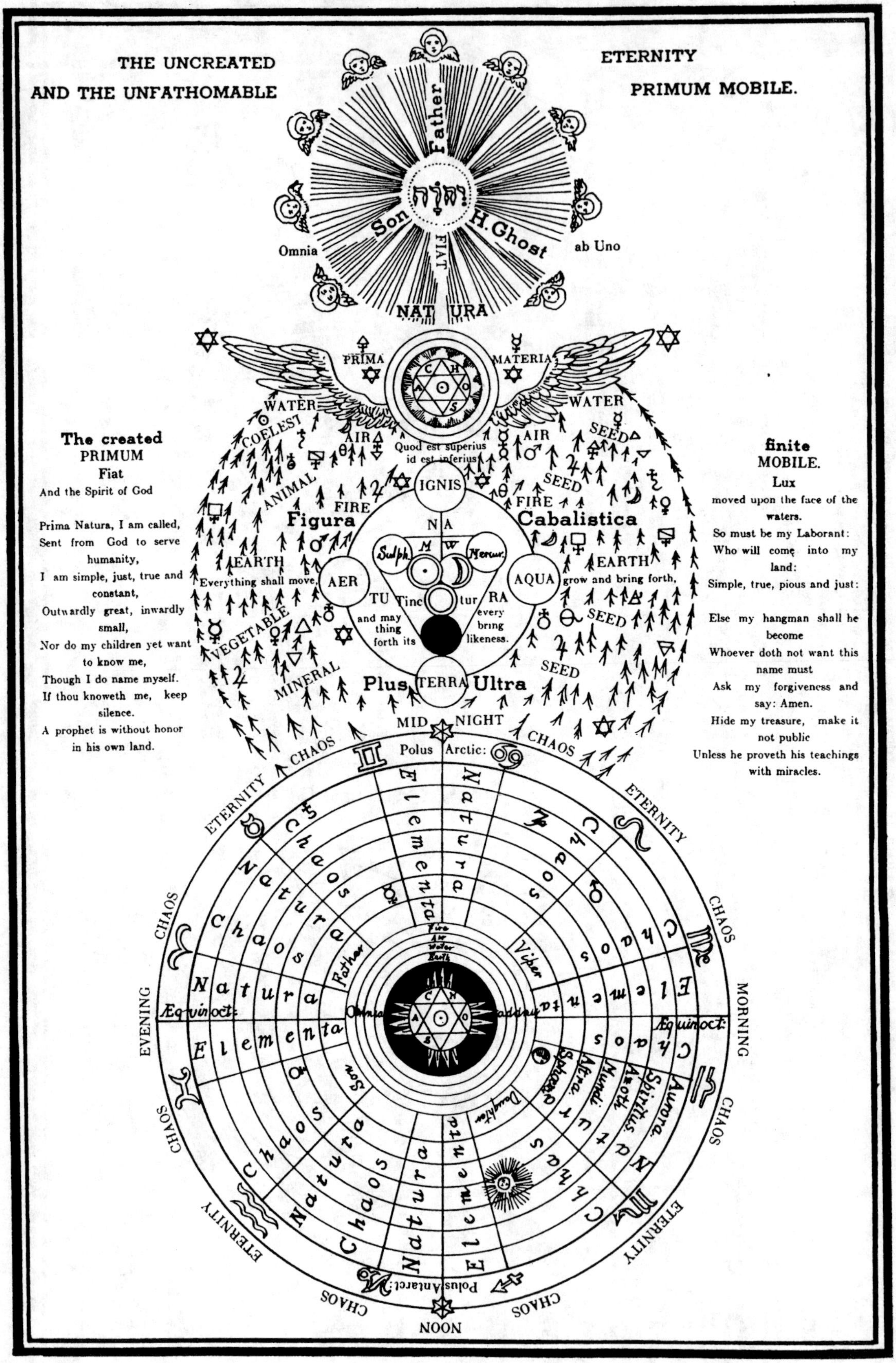
THE UNCREATED
AND THE UNFATHOMABLE
ETERNITY
PRIMUM MOBILE.
Father
Son
H. Ghost
FIAT
Omnia
ab Uno
NAT URA
PRIMA
MATERIA
WATER
COELEST
AIR
Quod est superius
id est inferius
SEED
ANIMAL
FIRE
IGNIS
Figura
Cabalistica
NA
Sulph.
Mercur.
EARTH
AER
AQUA
Everything shall move,
grow and bring forth,
TU
Tinc
tur
RA
and may thing forth its
every bring likeness.
VEGETABLE
MINERAL
Plus
TERRA
Ultra
MID
NIGHT
CHAOS
Polus Arctic:
The created
PRIMUM
Fiat
And the Spirit of God
Prima Natura, I am called,
Sent from God to serve humanity,
I am simple, just, true and constant,
Outwardly great, inwardly small,
Nor do my children yet want to know me,
Though I do name myself.
If thou knoweth me, keep silence.
A prophet is without honor in his own land.
finite
MOBILE.
Lux
moved upon the face of the waters.
So must be my Laborant:
Who will come into my land:
Simple, true, pious and just:
Else my hangman shall he become
Whoever doth not want this name must
Ask my forgiveness and say: Amen.
Hide my treasure, make it not public
Unless he proveth his teachings with miracles.
ETERNITY
Chaos
Natura
Elementa
Father
Viper
Fire
Air
Water
Earth
Omnia
Equinoct:
EVENING
MORNING
Son
Daughter
Sphaera
Astra
Mundi
Azoth
Spiritus
Aurora
Polus Antarct:
NOON